CELEBRATE!

The Holiday Cookbook

MINNETONKA, MINNESOTA

CELEBRATE!

The Holiday Cookbook

Printed in 2008.

8 9 10 11 12 / 12 11 10 09 08
© 2000 Cooking Club of America
ISBN 10: 1-58159-107-1
ISBN 13: 978-1-58159-107-1

Cooking Club of America
12301 Whitewater Drive
Minnetonka, MN 55343
www.cookingclub.com

Tom Carpenter
Creative Director

Jennifer Weaverling
Senior Book Development
Coordinator

Shari Gross
Book Production Coordinator

Laura Belpedio
Senior Book Development
Assistant

Becky Landes
Rebecca Gammelgaard
Book Design and Production

Mowers Photography
Commissioned Photography

Peter Bischoff
Photo Assistant

Lisa Golden Schroeder
Food Stylist

Liz Gibba
Pegi Lee
Susan Telleen
Assistant Food Stylists

CONTENTS

CELEBRATING THE HOLIDAYS
with Great Food!

Traditional
THANKSGIVING

Traditional
HANUKKAH

We call them, simply enough, The Holidays—that action-packed, ever-busy stretch of the year from Thanksgiving through New Year's. This special time bestows both blessings and challenges to we who love to entertain beautifully, cook creatively and eat well.

The blessings are easy to define: plenty of reasons to get together with family and friends, on both a casual and more formal basis, and share good food and good times.

But we all know the challenges as well. Too many social activities jam themselves into those six short weeks. When you're doing the cooking, you want to do a great job, but sometimes you just need the perfect idea, something new or different or inventive to try. Sometimes you even need the entire get-together planned out, food-wise.

That's why we at the Cooking Club of America created this book—*Celebrate! The Holiday Cookbook*. Included are detailed menus and complete recipes for 20 wonderful holiday get-togethers. Celebrating will be easier than ever when you're armed with the ideas (over 100 recipes) in this holiday cookbook.

Every holiday gathering described in this book is organized and laid out in detail for you—a picture of the feast, a complete menu, and all the recipes and details. You'll see almost all the dishes photographed individually, so you know what you're creating.

Start at Thanksgiving. You'll find a very traditional celebration, an alternative menu for the smaller gathering, and a meal the Pilgrims might have thought very different indeed.

Move on to Hanukkah. You don't have to be Jewish to celebrate the great food offered in both the traditional and modernized menus given. We've included an idea for Kwanzaa, too, another holiday that offers great tastes.

Of course, you'll find plenty of general seasonal, holiday celebrations—like holiday cookies, unbelievable desserts, a tea party and a wonderful appetizer buffet—to fun and informal gatherings, like a trim-the-tree party and a buffet to follow winter outdoor activities. Christmas itself gets plenty of attention, too, with dinners from the big and impressive to the laid-back and easygoing, and even a brunch.

Finally we bring you New Year's. Try a romantic dinner for two, a family meal where everyone gets in the act of creating it, and menus for New Year's day activities too.

NEW YEAR'S EVE
for Two

We hope you take these menus to heart, and find some new and complete ideas to put to work making your holiday celebrations better than ever. But we also know everyone has their own traditions, and those are important too. In that case, we think you'll find plenty of recipe gems which you can incorporate into what you already do during the holidays.

Either way, it's time to celebrate—The Holidays, of course, but also the fact that you now have a cookbook to help you through them.

Holiday
COOKIES

CHRISTMAS
Brunch

Alternative
THANKSGIVING

by Mary Evans

Who says you have to squeeze 23 people into your dining room, living room, kitchen and hallway to have a proper Thanksgiving? A smaller group, and a more intimate setting, can be just as satisfying...and is certainly more relaxing for the cook!

This simple but elegant menu borrows elements of a more traditional meal and makes them smaller and easier to make...

Alternative
THANKSGIVING

MENU

MAPLE-BALSAMIC GLAZED
TURKEY BREAST

TWICE-BAKED SWEET POTATOES

WILD RICE AND
DRIED CRANBERRY PILAF

CARAMEL-PECAN TARTS

Serves 4

but equally as satisfying and delicious. You can make the wild rice and sweet potatoes ahead of time. And you'll love the way the white turkey breast slices are offset by the rich, brown-basted skin; add your favorite stuffing recipe and enjoy!

MAPLE-BALSAMIC GLAZED TURKEY BREAST

Basting Sauce

3	tablespoons balsamic vinegar
5	teaspoons maple syrup
5	teaspoons Dijon mustard
1	tablespoon butter
1½	teaspoons chopped fresh rosemary
¼	teaspoon salt
⅛	teaspoon freshly ground pepper

Turkey

	3-to 5-lb. turkey breast
1½	cups canned reduced-sodium chicken broth
2	tablespoons all-purpose flour

1. Heat oven to 325°F. In small saucepan, heat vinegar, syrup, mustard, butter, rosemary, salt and pepper over low heat until butter is melted. Reserve 1 tablespoon basting sauce.

2. Place turkey breast in shallow roasting pan; brush with basting sauce. Bake uncovered 1½ to 2 hours, basting occasionally, until internal temperature reaches 180°F and skin is a deep mahogany brown. Remove to carving board; let rest while preparing gravy.

3. Add 1 cup of the chicken broth to roasting pan along with reserved basting sauce; place over medium heat and bring to a boil, stirring in any browned bits and roasting juices. Whisk remaining ½ cup broth with flour. Whisk into pan; continue cooking until gravy has thickened. Carve breast. Serve with gravy.

4 servings

Maple-Balsamic Glazed Turkey Breast

*Feel free to substitute four Cornish game hens for the turkey breast. Roast
approximately 1½ hours or until juices run clear from the inner thigh.*

Maple-Balsamic Glazed Turkey Breast, Twice-Baked Sweet Potatoes, and Wild Rice and Dried Cranberry Pilaf

TWICE-BAKED SWEET POTATOES

This recipe gives twice-baked potatoes a new twist and avoids the candied toppings usually found on sweet potatoes.

2   sweet potatoes (about ¾-lb.)
1   tablespoon butter
2   tablespoons sour cream
1   egg, lightly beaten
½   cup freshly grated Parmesan cheese
¼   teaspoon freshly grated nutmeg
⅛   teaspoon freshly ground pepper

1. Heat oven to 400°F.

2. Prick sweet potatoes with fork; bake 1 to 1¼ hours or until tender.

3. Let potatoes cool to lukewarm; cut in half. Remove flesh and place in medium bowl, leaving about ¼-inch shell.

4. Mash potato with butter; stir in sour cream, egg, Parmesan, nutmeg and pepper. Scoop mixture into shell halves. Potatoes can be prepared up to one day ahead, to this point. Cover and refrigerate.

5. Heat oven to 350°F. Place potatoes on baking sheet. Bake 30 minutes or until heated through.

4 servings

WILD RICE AND DRIED CRANBERRY PILAF

Yellow squash, dried cranberries and green onion tops brighten the earth tones of wild rice.

1   bunch green onions
2   tablespoons butter
2   cups canned reduced-sodium chicken broth
¾   cup wild rice*
½   cup diced yellow squash
½   cup dried cranberries

1. Chop white portion of green onions; reserve green portions.

2. In large saucepan, heat 1 tablespoon of the butter over medium heat until sizzling. Add chopped onion; sauté 3 to 4 minutes or until softened. Add chicken broth; bring to a boil.

3. Rinse wild rice; add to broth. Reduce heat to low. Cover and simmer 45 to 60 minutes or until rice is tender.

4. Meanwhile, heat remaining tablespoon butter in medium skillet. Add squash; sauté 3 minutes.

5. Chop tender parts of reserved green onion portions; add ¼ cup to squash. Continue to cook about 2 minutes or until squash is crisp-tender. Stir vegetables and cranberries into rice.

4 servings

CARAMEL-PECAN TARTS

These wonderful tarts will make you thankful indeed. Caramel and pecans bake in a buttery crust for a fitting end to this bountiful day.

Caramel-Pecan Tart

Crust
- 1 cup all-purpose flour
- ¼ teaspoon salt
- 6 tablespoons butter, chilled, cut up
- 1 egg yolk

Filling
- ¼ cup butter
- ¼ cup sugar
- ¼ cup packed brown sugar
- ¼ cup corn syrup
- ¼ cup heavy whipping cream
- 1 cup pecan halves
- 1 teaspoon vanilla

1. Heat oven to 400°F. Place flour and salt in medium bowl. Cut in butter until mixture crumbles. Stir in egg yolk; work mixture together with hands to blend well and form dough.

2. Divide mixture into 4 pieces. Press each piece over bottom and up sides of 4 (4½-inch) individual fluted tart pans with removable bottoms. Place on aluminum foil-lined baking sheet. Bake 5 to 8 minutes or until crust is golden brown and set. Let cool on baking sheet. Reduce heat to 350°F.

3. Combine butter, sugar, brown sugar and corn syrup in medium saucepan. Heat over low heat until butter is melted; increase heat to medium and cook about 5 minutes, stirring constantly, until mixture comes to a full boil. Stir in cream and pecans; boil 1 minute. Remove from heat; stir in vanilla. Pour into tart shells. Bake 20 to 25 minutes or until filling darkens, thickens and reduces. Cool to lukewarm or completely cool.

4 servings

ALL ABOUT TARTS

Tarts make wonderful alternatives to a traditional, double-crusted pie. Why go with a tart? First, a tart is simple to make, with only one pastry crust and shallow sides. Two, the exposed top allows the filling—in this case a heavenly caramel-pecan mix—to be the taste star. Three—because you use less filling than a pie would command, there's less chance for a soggy crust. Finally, a tart is easy to serve, and just seems to have extra appetite appeal with its wide-open display of the crust-cradled goodies.

You'll want to invest in tart pans, which come in a variety of shapes and sizes. Good kitchen supply stores will carry a nice selection, and you can look on-line as well.

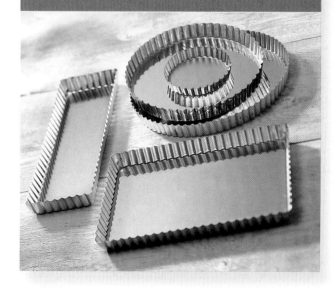

*RICE TIP

Rice can be prepared up to 2 days ahead. Cover cooked, cooled rice and refrigerate. Reheat over low heat, stirring occasionally, adding a bit of water or broth if necessary to prevent scorching.

Vegetarian
THANKSGIVING
by Mary Evans

Vegetarian
THANKSGIVING

MENU

WILD MUSHROOM
AND LEEK STROGANOFF

GARLIC AND
ROSEMARY MASHED POTATOES

BAKED WINTER SQUASH
WITH SAGE CORNBREAD TOPPING

PEAR AND CANDIED PECAN SALAD

CRANBERRY-ORANGE
CREME BRULEE

Serves 8

Attendees at the original Thanksgiving Banquet may not have dreamed of a meatless meal, but had the hunters not had any success with wild turkey, deer, duck or other game, a menu like this probably would have been readily accepted! The ingredients are robust, the tastes savory.

And, too often, vegetarians are left out on this turkey-focused day. So, we've taken traditional components and put them together in satisfying, meatless ways. You'll leave the table counting your blessings. For hosts or hostesses blending vegetarians and nonvegetarians alike, try combining some or all of these menu items with others to please all your guests.

WILD MUSHROOM AND LEEK STROGANOFF

You'll find yourself using this fabulous recipe repeatedly. Served here with mashed potatoes as befits a Thanksgiving feast, it is equally good tossed with pasta. To simplify Thanksgiving day, prepare the stroganoff in advance and reheat before serving.

- 3 tablespoons vegetable oil
- 1 lb. leeks, roots and coarse green sections trimmed, cut in ¼-inch slices
- 8 oz. white mushrooms, quartered
- 6 oz. portobello mushrooms, cut into ¾-inch pieces
- 3 oz. shiitake mushrooms, stems removed, quartered
- 3 oz. oyster mushrooms, coarsely chopped
- 1 cup red wine
- ¼ cup Madeira wine
- 2 tablespoons tomato paste
- ½ teaspoon salt
- ⅛ teaspoon freshly ground pepper

1. Heat oil in Dutch oven or large pot over low heat until hot. Add leeks; sauté 10 minutes or until tender. Add mushrooms; increase heat to medium. Cook 5 minutes, stirring frequently.

2. Stir in red wine, Madeira, tomato paste, salt and pepper; bring to a boil. Reduce heat to low; cover and simmer 15 minutes.

3. Remove cover and simmer an additional 15 minutes, stirring occasionally. Serve over Garlic and Rosemary Mashed Potatoes.

8 servings

GARLIC AND ROSEMARY MASHED POTATOES

Garlic and rosemary team with goat cheese to create these incredibly flavorful mashed potatoes. For a milder flavor, substitute cream cheese for the goat cheese.

- 3 lb. Yukon Gold potatoes
- 15 garlic cloves, minced
- 1¾ teaspoons salt
- 4 oz. goat cheese
- 2 teaspoons chopped fresh rosemary
- ⅛ teaspoon pepper

1. Place potatoes, garlic and 1 teaspoon of the salt in Dutch oven or large pot with enough water to cover potatoes. Bring to a boil over medium-high heat; cook 30 minutes or until tender. Drain, reserving cooking liquid.

2. Return potatoes and garlic to pan. Mash, adding reserved cooking liquid as necessary, until smooth.

3. Stir in remaining ¾ teaspoon salt, goat cheese, rosemary and pepper. Mash until smooth. Serve with Wild Mushroom and Leek Stroganoff.

8 servings

ABOUT WINTER SQUASH

Winter squash are those that ripen with the cooler weather of autumn. Acorn squash is the most common winter squash, but other varieties include buttercup, butternut, Hubbard and spaghetti squash. Pumpkin is a winter squash as well. The common denominator of winter squashes: They have thick skins and need to be peeled before cooking, or long-baked (as in the Baked Winter Squash with Cornbread Topping recipe on page 19).

When buying winter squash at the farmers' market or store, look for squashes that are heavy and solid; stay away from ones with cracked skin, mushy spots or odd color patches. If a squash gets a nick in the skin, use it right away! All winter squashes store well for up to a month in a cool, dry place (not the refrigerator) before you eat them.

*Baked Winter
Squash with
Sage Cornbread
Topping*

*Garlic and
Rosemary
Mashed Potatoes*

*Wild Mushroom
and Leek
Stroganoff*

BAKED WINTER SQUASH WITH SAGE CORNBREAD TOPPING

No Thanksgiving menu is complete without stuffing. Here it is used as a topping for baked acorn squash. Feel free to prepare the cornbread topping ahead; bring to room temperature for about 2 hours before adding to the squash.

2 large (about 2 lb. each) acorn squash

Topping
  1 tablespoon vegetable oil
  ¼ cup butter
  ¾ cup chopped onion
  ¾ cup chopped celery
  2 teaspoons dry sage, crumbled
  ½ teaspoon salt
  ⅛ teaspoon freshly ground pepper
  5 cups dried cornbread cubes
  ½ cup vegetable broth or water

1. Heat oven to 375°F. Line 9x13-inch pan with aluminum foil; lightly oil.

2. Cut squash in half; place cut side down on pan. Bake 1 to 1¼ hours or until tender. Remove seeds and place cut side up on pan.

3. In large skillet, heat butter over low heat until melted. Add onion and celery; cook 8 to 10 minutes or until tender. Stir in sage, salt and pepper; add cornbread and toss to coat. Drizzle with vegetable broth.

4. Divide among cavities of squash; bake an additional 15 minutes or until topping is slightly browned. Cut each half in half and serve.

8 servings

Pear and Candied Pecan Salad

The pecans pack a zing that goes beautifully with the sweetness of pears and crunch of greens.

PEAR AND CANDIED PECAN SALAD

Candied Pecans

¼ cup sugar
½ teaspoon salt
¼ teaspoon cinnamon
¼ teaspoon ground ginger
¼ teaspoon freshly ground pepper
    Pinch cayenne
2 tablespoons butter
1½ cups pecan halves

Dressing

2 tablespoons cider vinegar
1 teaspoon Dijon mustard
1 teaspoon honey
¼ teaspoon cinnamon
¼ teaspoon salt
¼ teaspoon freshly ground pepper
6 tablespoons vegetable oil

Salad

8 cups mixed greens
2 ripe Anjou pears, sliced

1. In small bowl, mix together sugar, ½ teaspoon salt, ¼ teaspoon cinnamon, ginger, ¼ teaspoon pepper and cayenne.

2. In medium skillet, combine butter, sugar mixture and pecans. Heat over medium heat, stirring constantly, until sugar has melted and nuts are coated. Cool on lightly greased aluminum foil.

3. In small bowl, whisk together vinegar, mustard, honey, ¼ teaspoon cinnamon, ¼ teaspoon salt and ¼ teaspoon pepper. Slowly whisk in oil.

4. To serve, toss greens with dressing. Add pears and toss to coat. Sprinkle with pecans.

8 servings

CRANBERRY-ORANGE CREME BRULEE

The crunchy topping can be broiled a few hours in advance and refrigerated.

¾ cup cranberry juice concentrate
¼ cup orange liqueur
6 egg yolks
2 eggs
¾ cup sugar
2½ cups whipping cream
3 to 5 drops red food color
½ cup packed brown sugar

1. Heat oven to 325°F. Place 8 (6-oz.) custard cups in shallow pan. Bring large pot of water to a simmer.

2. In small saucepan over medium-high heat, bring cranberry juice concentrate to a boil; continue cooking about 5 minutes or until reduced to ¼ cup. Remove from heat; stir in orange liqueur.

3. In medium bowl, whisk together egg yolks and eggs. Slowly whisk in sugar. Stir in cream, then cranberry mixture. Stir in food color to turn mixture pink. Pour into custard cups. Place in oven; add simmering water until half way up sides of cups. Bake 40 to 45 minutes or until just set. Let cool 1 hour at room temperature. Refrigerate, covered, several hours.

4. Before serving, heat broiler. Place cups in shallow baking pan; top each with 1 tablespoon brown sugar. Place under broiler 4 to 6 inches from heat; broil 1 to 2 minutes or until brown sugar melts. Refrigerate leftovers.

8 servings

Traditional
THANKSGIVING

by Lisa Golden Schroeder

Once more a crisp autumn has arrived, along with our all-American seasonal feast. This annual celebration always gives us a chance to feature the unique cornucopia of fall produce available at its peak as the days grow shorter. While family favorites have first dibs on the holiday table, consider slipping in some variations on familiar themes. Of course, a golden roasted turkey reigns, but why not try a new glaze . . . some fresh rosemary, orange marmalade and cream sherry? Glistening cranberries cooked with dried figs and ginger pair beautifully with the roast turkey. Take a closer look at the world of root vegetables, tender and new this time of year. Celery root, winter squashes and parsnips may be daunting to look at, but once they're peeled and cooked the flavors are earthy and sweet. Winter pears poached in spicy syrup

Traditional
THANKSGIVING

MENU

ROSEMARY-ORANGE TURKEY

SOURDOUGH AND FENNEL
BREAD STUFFING

SMASHED POTATOES AND CELERY ROOT

CRANBERRY-FIG CHUTNEY

MAPLE-GLAZED VEGETABLES

SPINACH AND ROMAINE SALAD
WITH BALSAMIC-MARINATED ONIONS

SPICED POACHED PEARS

HONEY-HAZELNUT PUMPKIN PIE

Serves 8

are aromatic and luxurious, while a twist on pumpkin pie, rich with hazelnuts, will be asked for again and again.

This traditional Thanksgiving meal can be a handful to prepare, but with careful planning it will be much less stressful and always memorable!

Two weeks ahead:
- ■ Order fresh turkey, pick up 1 to 2 days before Thanksgiving.

The week before:
- ■ Make list of menu and serving pieces you'll need.
- ■ Make two grocery lists—one for perishables, one for nonperishable items.
- ■ Shop for nonperishables.
- ■ Clean out refrigerator to make room for food to come.
- ■ Organize all table-setting details—iron linens, make place cards, plan a kids' table.
- ■ Prepare and freeze Hazelnut-Honey Pumpkin Pie.
- ■ Prepare Candied Hazelnuts; store airtight.
- ■ Cut up and toast bread for stuffing.

Two days before:
- ■ Shop for perishable groceries.
- ■ Poach pears and chill in syrup.
- ■ Prepare Cranberry-Fig Chutney.

One day before:
- ■ Prepare Balsamic Vinaigrette and marinate onions; store in refrigerator.
- ■ Remove pie from freezer to thaw.
- ■ Cook potatoes and celery root; store in refrigerator.
- ■ Roast Maple-Glazed Vegetables.
- ■ Assemble stuffing; refrigerate.

Thanksgiving Day:
- ■ Set the table(s).
- ■ Roast turkey; make gravy.
- ■ Reheat potatoes and celery root—finish recipe.
- ■ Reheat Maple-Glazed Vegetables.
- ■ Toss salad.
- ■ Reduce poaching syrup for pears, if desired.
- ■ Whip cream for desserts.

Rosemary-Orange Turkey

Cream sherry is an unexpected and delicious ingredient in the glaze and gravy of this herb and citrus-scented roast turkey. Sherries are fortified wines originally made in Spain; cream sherry is older and darker than other sherry varieties and is quite sweet. Madeira wine could be substituted.

ROSEMARY-ORANGE TURKEY

Turkey
1 (12-lb.) turkey
3 tablespoons olive oil
2 oranges, cut into wedges
1 tablespoon kosher (coarse) salt
2 teaspoons freshly ground pepper
1 medium onion, cut into wedges
3 sprigs fresh rosemary
2 sprigs fresh thyme
2 to 3 cups chicken broth

Glaze
⅓ cup orange marmalade or apricot jam
3 tablespoons cream sherry
2 tablespoons orange juice
3 cloves garlic, minced
2 tablespoons butter, melted

Gravy
2 to 3 cups chicken broth
1 tablespoon chopped fresh rosemary
  or 2 teaspoons dried rosemary, crushed
½ cup cream sherry
3 tablespoons cornstarch
½ teaspoon salt
½ teaspoon freshly ground pepper

1. Heat oven to 400°F. Rinse turkey and pat dry. Tuck wing tips under turkey. Rub with oil, inside and out. Place on rack in large roasting pan. Squeeze juice from one-half of one orange over turkey. Season inside and out with salt and pepper. Place remaining orange wedges, onion, and sprigs of herbs inside turkey. Pour 2 cups broth into pan around turkey.

2. Bake 30 minutes. Cover loosely with aluminum foil. Reduce oven temperature to 325°F. Bake an additional 2 hours. Replenish broth in bottom of pan if broth has evaporated. Baste turkey with accumulated juices every 30 minutes. Meanwhile, combine all glaze ingredients in small bowl.

3. Uncover turkey; brush with glaze. Continue roasting another 30 minutes or until internal temperature reaches 180°F. (Insert instant-read thermometer in center of thigh near the body.) Let turkey stand 5 minutes. Carefully transfer to serving platter. Tent with foil; let rest while making gravy.

4. For gravy, pour juices from roasting pan into a 4-cup glass measure (scrape in browned bits from pan). Skim off and discard fat. Add additional broth to equal 3 cups. Pour pan juice-broth mixture into medium saucepan. Add rosemary and cream sherry. Combine cornstarch with ½ cup broth and stir into saucepan. Cook and stir over medium heat until thickened and bubbly; cook and stir for an additional 2 minutes. Season with salt and pepper.

8 servings

ROASTING TIPS

Start with a flavorful, moist bird. Local, free-range, organic turkeys are superb. If they are not available, look for fresh, unfrozen birds. If you use a frozen turkey, thaw it carefully in the refrigerator, allowing several days thawing time for large birds. Here are some additional tips:

❧ Leave the legs untied so the heat can reach the thigh meat quickly.

❧ Pour stock, water or wine on the bottom of the roasting pan; replenish it as needed while cooking. The moisture rises during roasting, keeping the meat and skin moist.

❧ Start with a high oven temperature (400°F) and roast the turkey for 30 minutes to begin browning the skin, then reduce the heat to 325°F for slower cooking. Loosely cover the bird with

foil during roasting to avoid excessive browning. Remove foil for final browning, near the end of the cooking time.

❧ Turkey should be cooked to an internal temperature of 180 to 185°F. Use a meat thermometer inserted into the center of the thigh near the body to check for doneness.

❧ Let the turkey sit loosely covered for 20 to 30 minutes before carving so the juices can resettle.

Traditional Thanksgiving

SOURDOUGH AND FENNEL BREAD STUFFING

Save the fennel fronds, the wispy leaves of fennel bulbs. Lightly aromatic, they are a ready-made garnish. This very moist stuffing is rich with vegetables and herbs. If you prefer a drier stuffing, reduce the amount of broth added to moisten the bread mixture.

10 cups (¾-inch) cubes sourdough bread (about 1-lb.)
½ cup butter
3 medium fennel bulbs, fronds removed, chopped
2 medium onions, chopped
3 ribs celery, sliced
1 tablespoon fennel seeds
2 large red bell peppers, chopped
1 tablespoon dried sage, crumbled
2 teaspoons dried thyme
2 teaspoons dried marjoram
¼ teaspoon salt
¼ teaspoon freshly ground pepper
1½ cups chicken broth
    Fresh fennel fronds, if desired

1. Heat oven to 400°F. Spread bread cubes on two baking sheets. Toast 10 minutes or until lightly browned, stirring occasionally. Transfer to large bowl.

2. In Dutch oven, melt butter over medium-high heat. Add fennel bulbs, onions, celery and fennel seeds. Sauté about 15 minutes or until vegetables are tender and golden brown. Reduce heat to medium; add bell peppers, sage, thyme and marjoram. Sauté an additional 10 minutes or until peppers are tender. Season with salt and pepper. Stir vegetable mixture into bread cubes; mix well.

3. Heat oven to 350°F. Moisten stuffing mixture with chicken broth. Butter baking pan; spoon stuffing into pan. Cover mixture with buttered aluminum foil, buttered side down; bake 30 minutes or until heated through. Uncover and bake an additional 20 minutes or until top is just crisp and golden. Garnish with chopped fresh fennel fronds.

10 servings

SMASHED POTATOES AND CELERY ROOT

The scruffy appearance of untrimmed celery root (celeriac) belies its delicate flavor—a cross between celery and walnuts. Use a large knife to peel away its heavy, rough skin. Crème fraîche is a thick, tangy cream with a velvety smooth texture. It's available in the dairy section of the grocery, but if it's difficult to find, substitute whipping cream. Be sure to freshly grate the nutmeg (use a small nutmeg grater or shaver or the finest shred on a box grater); its subtle spiciness will be fresher and lighter than purchased ground nutmeg.

2 lb. Yukon Gold potatoes, peeled,
    cut into 1-inch pieces
1 medium celery root (celeriac)
    (about 2 lb.), peeled, cut into 1-inch pieces
1½ teaspoons kosher (coarse) salt
1 cup crème fraîche or whipping cream*
¾ teaspoon freshly grated nutmeg,
    plus more if needed
½ teaspoon freshly ground pepper
½ teaspoon chopped fresh parsley

1. Place vegetables in Dutch oven; cover with water. Add 1 teaspoon of the salt. Bring to a boil; reduce heat and simmer 20 to 25 minutes or until vegetables are very tender. Drain well.

2. Return cooked vegetables to Dutch oven. Stir in crème fraîche, remaining ½ teaspoon salt, nutmeg and pepper. Lightly smash vegetables with potato masher. Spoon into warmed serving dish; sprinkle with parsley.

8 servings

*TIP

For a lighter version of Smashed Potatoes and Celery Root, mash vegetables and stir in buttermilk or some light sour cream and nonfat milk until desired consistency.

Cranberry-Fig Chutney

CRANBERRY-FIG CHUTNEY

This is a part of the holiday menu that really benefits from being prepared ahead so the flavors can blend and develop. Prepare up to four days ahead.

1 (12-oz.) bag fresh cranberries (3 cups)
1 cup chopped dried Black Mission figs
½ cup finely chopped onion
¾ cup packed brown sugar
1¾ cups apple juice
3 tablespoons cider vinegar
1½ tablespoons finely chopped or grated fresh ginger

1. In large saucepan, combine cranberries, figs, onion, brown sugar, juice, vinegar and ginger; mix well. Bring to a boil over medium-high heat. Reduce heat to medium-low. Simmer uncovered about 20 to 25 minutes, stirring frequently, until cranberries pop and sauce is thickened. (Sauce will thicken as it cools.)

2. Cool mixture. Cover and store in refrigerator until serving.*

3 cups

*TIP

If chutney is too thick when chilled, stir in more apple juice until you get the desired consistency.

DON'T THINK OF LEFTOVERS; THINK OF MEAL STARTERS.

If there are any leftovers from this fabulous meal, you know they won't go to waste. However, some ingenuity may be required to get everyone excited about seeing them again, so here are some quick ways to satisfy.

- Toss chopped roasted turkey with some hot cooked rigatoni pasta, extra gravy and diced tomatoes to make a ragoût.

- Create an "à la king" mixture with gravy and chopped turkey; spoon over mashed potato pancakes or baked potatoes.

- Make melted cheese panini sandwiches. Split focaccia bread, spread with cream cheese, cranberry chutney, sliced turkey and cheddar cheese; broil until cheese is melted.

- Soft tacos or tostada salads are great with chopped turkey, salsa, guacamole, beans and fresh cilantro.

- Try turkey hash: chopped turkey, cubed potatoes, chili powder and garlic; sauté together and top with poached eggs and salsa verde.

MAPLE-GLAZED VEGETABLES

Because these vegetables need a hotter oven than the turkey, roast them ahead of time, unless you have two ovens. Cover and refrigerate until ready to serve. To reheat, arrange vegetables on a heatproof platter and heat in a 350°F oven until hot, brushing with more maple syrup if desired.

1   large (2½ lb.) butternut or other hard winter squash, peeled, cut into 3-inch chunks
5   large carrots, peeled, cut into 3-inch chunks
4   large parsnips, peeled, cut into 3-inch chunks
2   tablespoons olive oil
2   tablespoons unsalted butter, melted
½   teaspoon kosher (coarse) salt
½   teaspoon freshly ground nutmeg
½   cup maple syrup

1. Heat oven to 425°F. Line two baking sheets with aluminum foil; arrange vegetables on baking sheets.

2. Stir together oil, butter, salt, nutmeg and syrup. Brush vegetables with glaze. Bake 35 to 40 minutes or until very tender and browned.

8 servings

Maple-Glazed Vegetables

SPINACH AND ROMAINE SALAD WITH BALSAMIC-MARINATED ONIONS

Marinating the onions not only makes them crisp-tender, but also further flavors the vinaigrette dressing. Winter grapefruit partners well with hearty greens, and you could also add other winter fruit such as blood oranges or starfruit.

3   medium pink grapefruit
⅓   cup red or white balsamic vinegar
¼   cup walnut oil or extra-virgin olive oil
3   tablespoons honey
½   teaspoon freshly ground pepper
1   red onion, thinly sliced
8   cups baby spinach and romaine leaves
    Seeds of 1 pomegranate*

1. Slice peel from grapefruit with sharp knife. Cut between membranes to remove fruit segments, catching juices in glass measuring cup. Pour ¼ cup of the grapefruit juice into small bowl; place remaining grapefruit in another bowl and refrigerate.

2. In small bowl, whisk vinegar, oil, honey and pepper into grapefruit juice until smooth. Add onions to vinaigrette. Cover and let stand at least 1 hour.

3. Just before serving, place spinach, romaine, grape-fruit segments and pomegranate seeds in large salad bowl. Remove onions from vinaigrette; toss with salad mixture. Spoon remaining vinaigrette over salad; toss to coat. Serve immediately.

8 servings

*TIP

To easily seed a pomegranate, cut in half. Under slowing running cold water, break halves into pieces and remove seeds.

Spinach and Romaine Salad with Balsamic-Marinated Onions

SPICED POACHED PEARS

The exotic flavor of these pears is easily achieved using a blend of whole spices steeped in the poaching syrup. The spicy flavor is intensified by reducing the poaching liquid before serving the dessert. For a really pretty presentation, use the small Seckel pears available this time of year. Double the number of pears you poach (there should be enough poaching liquid) and serve them in a large glass bowl on a buffet, along with the Honey Hazelnut Pumpkin Pie (page 33). Offer softly whipped cream to spoon onto the pears or the pie.

Syrup

  8 cups water
  2 cups sugar
  1 vanilla bean, split lengthwise,
      or ½ teaspoon vanilla
  5 whole cardamom pods
  2 (3-inch) cinnamon sticks
  ¼ teaspoon black peppercorns
  ⅛ teaspoon anise seeds

Pears

  8 medium firm-ripe pears (Bosc, Anjou)
  1 lemon, halved
      Raspberry or chocolate sorbet

1. In large Dutch oven or pot, combine water, sugar, vanilla, cardamom, cinnamon, peppercorns and anise. Bring mixture to a simmer over medium-low heat.

2. Peel each pear, leaving stem. Core pears through bottom with apple corer or small melon baller. As you work, rub pears with lemon halves (or place in bowl of water with some lemon juice) to prevent browning.

3. Add pears to syrup. Keep heat low so syrup is just simmering. Poach pears, covered, 20 to 25 minutes or until tender. Cool pears in syrup. This can be prepared up to 3 days ahead. Refrigerate pears in syrup.

4. To serve, remove pears from syrup and set aside. Strain syrup through a wire mesh sieve back into Dutch oven. Bring to a boil; boil uncovered about 45 minutes or until syrup is reduced to about 3 cups. The syrup should be light-amber colored, slightly thickened and syrupy.

5. Place each pear in dessert bowl. Place small scoops of sorbet next to pears; spoon spiced syrup over pears.

Blushing Spiced Pears

1. Poach pears in spiced syrup as directed above. Chill pears in syrup. Omit step to reduce syrup. Remove pears from syrup and serve with sorbet, drizzled with crème de cassis (blackberry brandy), framboise (raspberry liqueur), or raspberry coffee syrup.

8 servings

*H*oney-Hazelnut Pumkin Pie could also be transformed into a tart by using a deep 10-inch tart tin with a removable rim. The honey in this silky filling will make the custard a little softer than a standard pumpkin pie. Make the candied hazelnuts ahead of time and store airtight—they're great on ice cream too.

HONEY-HAZELNUT PUMPKIN PIE

Crust

⅓ cup toasted hazelnuts*
1¼ cups all-purpose flour
¼ cup sugar
½ cup butter, chilled, cut up
1 egg yolk

Filling

1 (16-oz.) can pumpkin
½ cup honey
¼ cup hazelnut liqueur (or hazelnut-flavored liquid
    coffee creamer or coffee syrup)
¾ teaspoon salt
¼ teaspoon ground nutmeg
4 eggs
¾ cup evaporated milk
    Whipped cream
    Candied Hazelnuts

Candied Hazelnuts

1 cup toasted chopped hazelnuts
¾ cup sugar
½ teaspoon cinnamon
¼ teaspoon ground ginger
⅛ teaspoon ground cloves

1. To prepare crust in food processor, finely chop hazelnuts with flour and sugar. Add butter; process until mixture crumbles. Add egg yolk; process until dough holds together. Press dough evenly into 10-inch pie plate. Crimp edge of dough with tines of fork. Refrigerate 30 minutes or until dough is firm.

2. Heat oven to 375°F. In large bowl, combine pumpkin, honey, liqueur, salt, and nutmeg; whisk in eggs until well blended. Whisk in evaporated milk until mixture is smooth. Pour into pastry crust.

3. Bake 55 to 60 minutes or until knife tip inserted near edge of pie comes out clean. Cool completely on wire rack. Serve topped with whipped cream and Candied Hazelnuts.

4. To prepare hazelnuts, line baking sheet with aluminum foil. Combine hazelnuts, sugar, cinnamon, ginger and cloves in heavy medium skillet. Cook over medium heat, stirring constantly until sugar melts. Continue to cook and stir until sugar is dark-amber and nuts are coated. Pour mixture onto baking sheet, spreading mixture as thinly as possible. Cool completely. Break caramelized nuts into large pieces to garnish slices of pie.

10 servings

✿ TIP

To toast nuts, heat oven to 350°F. Place hazelnuts in pie plate; toast in oven 5 to 10 minutes or until skins crack and nuts are fragrant. Pour nuts onto clean cloth dish towel; fold towel around nuts and rub vigorously to remove most of the dark skin (some skin will remain on nuts).

KWANZAA

by Charla Draper

Kwanzaa was a new and little-known observance when it appeared on the chronicle of holidays in the 60's. Created by Maulana (Ron) Karenga, Chairman of Black Studies at California State University, Kwanzaa was an element of the cultural renaissance

KWANZAA

MENU

OKRA CORN SALAD
WITH MUSTARD VINAIGRETTE

GROUNDNUT STEW

SAVORY CORNMEAL MUFFINS

COCONUT CAKE

FESTIVE LEMONADE

Serves 6

and black pride that emerged in an era of significant change in American society. Karenga's goal in creating the holiday was to recognize the culture of African-Americans and create a link with African peoples and traditions.

ABOUT KWANZAA

Kwanzaa is a unique holiday. It is not linked to religious, political or heroic individuals or deeds. Kwanzaa is a celebration of culture, community and family. Celebrated December 26 through January 1, it is based on seven principles. Each day during Kwanzaa, one of the principles is the focus of the day's activities. During the series of days, a family member or friend lights one of seven candles, each representing one principle. This person also starts a discussion of the day's principle. The principles are:

🌾 Umoja [oo-MOH-JAH] (Unity) To strive for and maintain unity within the family, community, nation and race.

🌾 Kujichagulia [koo-ji-chah-goo-LEE-ah] (Self-determination) To define ourselves, name ourselves, create for ourselves and speak for ourselves instead of being defined, named, created for and spoken for by others.

🌾 Ujima [oo-JEE-mah] (Collective work and responsibility) To build and maintain our community together, and to make our sisters' and brothers' problems our problems, and to solve them together.

🌾 Ujamma [oo-jah-MAH] (Cooperative economics) To build and maintain our own stores, shops and other businesses and to profit from them together.

🌾 Nia [NEE-ah] (Purpose) To make our collective vocation the building and developing of our communities in order to restore our people to their traditional greatness.

🌾 Kuumba [koo-OO-mbah] (Creativity) To do always as much as we can, in whatever way we can, in order to leave our community more beautiful and beneficial than we inherited it.

🌾 Imani [ee-MAH-nee] (Faith) To believe with all our heart in our people, our parents, our teachers, our leaders and in the righteousness and victory of our struggle.

Okra Corn Salad with Mustard Vinaigrette

OKRA CORN SALAD WITH MUSTARD VINAIGRETTE

Okra, often prepared as a hot vegetable side dish or ingredient in gumbo, is linked in this salad with corn and lettuce. Okra's unique properties contribute texture and viscosity to the vinaigrette.

    4   cups cold water
    2   cups frozen cut okra
    2   cups whole kernel corn, cooked
  1/2   cup chopped red bell pepper
  1/3   cup chopped green onion
  1/4   cup canola oil
    2   tablespoons balsamic vinegar
    2   teaspoons mustard
    1   teaspoon celery seed
  1/4   teaspoon salt
    4   cups iceberg lettuce

1. In 2-quart saucepan, bring cold water to a boil. Add okra; boil 45 to 60 seconds. Drain; rinse immediately with cold water.

2. In medium bowl, combine okra, corn, bell pepper and onion. Set aside.

3. In small container with air-tight lid, combine oil, vinegar, mustard, celery seed and salt. With lid tightly secured, shake mixture vigorously. Pour oil mixture over okra; toss. Cover; chill several hours or overnight. Serve over iceberg lettuce.

8 servings

GROUNDNUT STEW

In West Africa, peanuts, known as groundnuts, are often used in soups, stews and side dishes. This version of groundnut stew is flavored with peanut butter and garnished with nuts.

1½ lb. boneless skinless chicken breast, cut into 1-inch pieces
2 teaspoons chili powder
½ teaspoon freshly ground pepper
¼ teaspoon seasoned salt
2 tablespoons vegetable oil
1 cup chopped onion
1 teaspoon minced garlic
1½ cups chicken broth
½ cups sweet potato slices, halved
1 (14½ oz.) can diced tomatoes
⅓ cup peanut butter
2 tablespoons cold water
1 tablespoon cornstarch
  Cooked white rice
  Chopped cilantro
  Chopped peanuts

1. In medium bowl, combine chicken, chili powder, pepper and salt, mixing until chicken is thoroughly coated. Set aside.

2. In 4-quart Dutch oven, heat oil over medium heat until hot. Cook onion and garlic in oil, stirring occasionally, until onions are translucent. Add chicken; cook over medium-high heat, stirring frequently, until chicken is no longer pink in center. Add broth and sweet potatoes.

3. Reduce heat to low. Cover; simmer 10 minutes. Stir in tomatoes and peanut butter. Cover; simmer

Groundnut Stew

10 minutes. In small bowl, stir together water and cornstarch. Stir cornstarch mixture into chicken mixture. Continue cooking an additional 5 to 7 minutes or until mixture thickens slightly. Serve over hot, cooked rice. Garnish with cilantro and peanuts.

6 servings

Savory Cornmeal Muffins

SAVORY CORNMEAL MUFFINS

An ear of corn, representing the product of unified effort, is often displayed among the fruits and vegetables on the Kwanzaa table. These cornmeal based muffins are flavored with curry and ginger for a savory compliment to Groundnut Stew.

1 cup cornmeal
1 (8½ oz.) pkg. corn muffin mix
1 tablespoon baking powder
1½ teaspoons curry powder
1 teaspoon ginger
1 teaspoon salt
1 cup milk
2 eggs, beaten
¼ cup butter, melted
½ cup raisins

1. Heat oven to 400°F. Spray 12 muffin cups with nonstick cooking spray.

2. In medium bowl, stir together cornmeal, muffin mix, baking powder, curry powder, ginger and salt. Combine milk and eggs; add to cornmeal mixture, mixing just until blended. Stir in butter and raisins.

3. Spoon batter evenly into muffin cups. Bake 20 to 25 minutes or until golden brown.

12 muffins

Coconut Cake

KWANZAA TRADITIONS AND FOODS

In setting the Kwanzaa table, customary elements include a straw mat, candle holder or kinara for seven candles (see sidebar "About Kwanzaa"), a variety of fruits and vegetables, ears of corn, gifts that are handmade, and a communal libation cup.

As with many holidays, food is a key ingredient in the festivities. The term Kwanzaa is derived from the Swahili word kwaknza, which means "first" or "first fruits of the harvest." During the seven days of Kwanzaa, menus may include some of the foodstuffs native to the African diaspora: peanuts, okra, yams, black-eyed peas, corn and coconut. The observance concludes with a feast or karamu (kah-RAH-moo) on January 1st.

The feast on the final day of Kwanzaa can be planned as potluck where everyone contributes, or a single host or hostess can prepare each dish. The karamu menu may include traditional dishes and foods from Africa, the Caribbean or South America, representing the link among countries populated at one time by slaves from Africa.

Today Kwanzaa is celebrated by millions of people each year who welcome the holiday and opportunities it brings for fellowship among community, friends and family. And that's something anybody can celebrate!

COCONUT CAKE

Always a holiday favorite, this coconut cake includes almond flour, which contributes a nutty richness to the flavor profile.

Cake
1 ⅓   cups sugar
1   cup butter, softened
3   eggs
1   teaspoon vanilla
1 ⅓   cups all-purpose flour
⅔   cup almond flour
2   teaspoons baking powder
½   teaspoon salt
½   cup half-and-half

Frosting
⅓   cup water
2   egg whites
1 ¼   cups sugar
¼   teaspoon cream of tartar
1   teaspoon vanilla
2   cups sweetened coconut flakes

1. Heat oven to 350°F. Spray 13x9-inch pan with nonstick cooking spray; lightly flour.

2. In large bowl, cream sugar and butter until light and fluffy. Add eggs one at a time, beating well after each addition. Add vanilla; mix until blended. Combine flour, almond flour, baking powder and salt; add alternately with half-and-half, mixing until blended.

3. Spread batter evenly in pan. Bake 25 to 35 minutes or until toothpick inserted in center comes out clean. Cool 10 minutes; loosen from sides of pan. Invert onto cooling rack.

4. To prepare frosting, heat water in top of double boiler to simmer. Beat egg whites, sugar, cream of tartar and vanilla into water, beating about 7 minutes or until soft peaks form. Remove pan from heat. Cool 15 to 20 minutes. Spread frosting on top and sides. Sprinkle coconut on top and sides; pat gently into frosting.

16 servings

Festive Lemonade

FESTIVE LEMONADE

A refreshing and light libation, the addition of seltzer gives this thirst-quencher a festive touch.

½   cup water
1   cup sugar
¼   cup thinly sliced lemon peel
⅔   cup fresh lemon juice
1   quart natural or lemon-flavored seltzer*
    Lemon and lime slices

1. In 1-quart saucepan, combine water, sugar and lemon peel; cook over medium heat until mixture comes to a boil. Continue boiling 5 minutes. Remove from heat; stir in lemon juice. Cool; strain to remove lemon peel.

2. To serve, pour lemon juice mixture into 1½-quart pitcher; stir in seltzer. Garnish each serving with lemon and lime slices, if desired.

About 6 servings

* TIP
For a sweeter flavor but fewer servings, substitute 3 cups seltzer for 1 quart seltzer; adjust ingredient amounts as needed, to fit your celebration size.

Traditional
HANUKKAH
by Ethel G. Hofman

The Jewish holiday of Hanukkah (Chanukah) is an eight-day festival commemorating a double miracle: In 165 BCE, a small band of Jewish patriots headed by Judas Maccabaeus and his four brothers defeated Antiochus IV and his mighty Syrian-Greek army. The temple, where jugs of oil had been desecrated, was rededicated, and the single untainted cruse of oil—enough for only one day—miraculously burned for eight while a runner went for new oil. The holiday was observed each year by kindling lights for eight days, and Hanukkah became known as the Festival of Lights. It is customary for children to receive gifts for Hanukkah. In Eastern Europe, families gathered on the fifth night and children were given Hanukkah gelt (money). Today, influenced by Christmas gift giving, children receive gifts other than money.

Traditional
HANUKKAH

MENU

CLASSIC POTATO LATKES

SEPHARDIC FRIED FISH

CHEDDAR CHEESE GELT

SIMPLE SUFGANIOT

STUFFED APRICOTS AND DATES

Serves 4

MENU SUGGESTIONS

Honeydew Wedges Garnished with Pomegranate Seeds

Crisp Baby Greens   Basket of Winter Fruits

Serve Classic Potato Latkes with Sour Cream
and Chunky Applesauce Toppings

Foods fried in oil are traditional, symbolizing the miracle of the oil. Latkes and sufganiot are typical Ashkenazi (Eastern European) dishes. Dairy and cheese dishes are also popular and can be traced to the story of Judith, one of the heroines in the Book of Judith of the Apocryhpha (about 6th century BCE). According to legend, Judith fed salty cheeses to Holofernes, the general of the enemy Nebuchadnezzar's army. When he became thirsty, she plied him with copious amounts of wine, which made him drunk. He was beheaded, and this led to a Jewish victory.

You don't have to be Jewish to enjoy the tastes of Hanukkah. Choose an evening and give this menu a try!

CLASSIC POTATO LATKES

Save time by using frozen chopped onion. The lemon juice keeps potatoes from discoloring so that when cooked, these latkes are snow-white and moist on the inside.

3 large baking potatoes, peeled (about 2 lb.)
1 tablespoon fresh lemon juice
¼ cup chopped onion
3 eggs, lightly beaten
⅓ cup all-purpose flour
1 tablespoon cornstarch
1 teaspoon salt
⅛ teaspoon white pepper
3 tablespoons finely snipped fresh dill, if desired
Vegetable oil

1. Coarsely grate potatoes using grater or food processor. Remove to clean kichen towel; roll and squeeze out as much liquid as possible. Transfer to bowl; toss with lemon juice.

2. Stir in onion, eggs, flour, cornstarch, salt, pepper and dill. Heat about ⅛-inch oil in large skillet over medium-high heat.

3. Slide rounded tablespoons of potato mixture into hot oil, making sure latkes do not touch. Press with back of spoon to flatten. Fry 2 to 3 minutes on each side until crisp and browned. Drain on paper towels. (Latkes can be prepared up to 1 hour in advance. Place uncovered on baking sheet in 250°F oven.)

About 20 latkes

SEPHARDIC FRIED FISH

Use a fish fillet (such as flounder or tilapia) which cooks quickly, rather than steaks such as halibut or tuna. The rule of thumb for fish cookery is 10 minutes cooking time per 1 inch of thickness.

⅓ cup milk
⅓ cup all-purpose flour
1½ teaspoons garlic powder
½ teaspoon salt
⅛ teaspoon white pepper
1 lb. fish fillets
Vegetable oil
Cider vinegar
Parsley sprigs

1. Pour milk into shallow dish. In separate shallow dish, combine flour, garlic powder, salt and pepper. Set aside.

2. Cut fillets into 4-inch pieces. Wash and pat dry with paper towels. Place fish in milk, turning to coat both sides. Let stand 5 minutes. Shake off excess milk; place in flour mixture, turning to coat thoroughly.

3. Heat oil in medium skillet over medium-high heat. To test oil temperature, place 1-inch piece of bread in oil; if it browns within 60 seconds, oil is hot enough. Add fish. Cook 2 minutes on each side or until crisp, browned, and fish flakes at thickest parts. Fish should be opaque. Drain on paper towels. Arrange on serving dish; sprinkle with vinegar. Garnish with parsley; serve warm or at room temperature.

4 servings

Classic Potato Latkes and Sephardic Fried Fish

HANUKKAH HISTORY

Hanukkah is an interesting mix of traditions. As described, the holiday primarily commemorates the Jewish victory over the goliath Syrian-Greek army, as well as the miracle of one day's oil burning for eight as the Temple was rededicated. But Hanukkah isn't described in the Torah (first five books of the Old Testament) because the event didn't happen until 165 BCE.

That Hanukkah is eight days long — the same as the Jewish harvest festival of Sukkot — may be no coincidence. Some scholars suspect that the "first" Hanukkah was a delayed Sukkot celebration; there's not much time to celebrate harvest when you're waging a war against a militarily superior enemy.

And why the Hanukkah lights? Ostensibly, because of the symbolism to the oil burning in the Temple's eternal flame. But history also points to mid-winter celebrations, of almost every ancient religion, that center around light — trying to call back the sun and longer, warmer days once again.

There is probably truth in all these theories, which makes Hanukkah a meaningful holiday to celebrate with good food and family no matter what your religion. It's a celebration of light in the dark winter, of standing up for what you believe in, and of winning against all odds.

Traditional Hanukkah

CHEDDAR CHEESE GELT

In simpler times, children received gelt (Yiddish for money) in the form of coins as a Hanukkah gift. This recipe is a delicious, edible interpretation—one that's easy enough for children to make. With little adult supervision needed other than placing baking sheets in the oven, Cheddar Cheese Gelt can be part of your Hanukkah tradition.

1 (17¼-oz.) pkg. frozen puff pastry sheets, thawed
¼ cup mayonnaise
    Lemon pepper seasoning
    Paprika
⅓ cup finely shredded cheddar cheese

1. Heat oven to 400°F. Separate pastry sheets. Cut each sheet in half; press out any perforations with your fingers.

2. Spread each pastry portion with 1 tablespoon of the mayonnaise, to within ½ inch of edges. Sprinkle lightly with lemon pepper, paprika and 1½ tablespoons of the shredded cheese. Moisten one long edge with a little water. Roll up tightly as for a jellyroll, rolling towards the moist edge. Press gently to seal. Cut in ¼-inch slices and place on ungreased baking sheet. Press with knife blade to flatten slightly. Repeat with remaining pastry. Bake 7 minutes or until puffed and golden. Heat broiler. Place baking sheet 4 to 6 inches from broiler 1 to 2 minutes or until pastry is browned and slightly crisp.

7 dozen appetizers

SIMPLE SUFGANIOT

These Israeli-style jelly doughnuts are quick and easy because the raising agent is baking powder instead of yeast. If you don't have buttermilk, add 1½ teaspoons white vinegar or lemon juice to milk and let it stand at room temperature 15 minutes without stirring.

2 cups all-purpose flour
2 tablespoons sugar
4 teaspoons baking powder
3 tablespoons butter, cut in 3 pieces
¾ to 1 cup buttermilk
½ teaspoon vanilla
    Fruit preserves
    Vegetable oil
    Powdered sugar
    Cinnamon sugar

1. Place flour, sugar, baking powder and butter in food processor. Process until mixture resembles coarse bread crumbs.

2. In small bowl, stir together ¾ cup buttermilk with vanilla; add to flour mixture and process, adding buttermilk 1 teaspoon at a time if needed, to make a soft dough. Turn out onto floured surface; pat dough to ¼ inch thickness. Cut into circles using 1½-inch cookie cutter or top of small juice glass. Place ½ teaspoon preserves in center of each circle. Moisten edges with water, top with another circle. Press edges to seal.

3. In large saucepan, heat about 2 inches oil to 350°F. Gently slide sufganiot into hot oil. Fry over medium heat 2 to 3 minutes on each side, turning often to brown evenly. Drain on several thick paper towels. Roll in powdered sugar or cinnamon sugar while hot. Serve immediately.

About 20 sufganiot

STUFFED APRICOTS AND DATES

Prepare these several days ahead. Wrap tightly in plastic wrap and refrigerate.

¼ cup unsalted pistachios
⅓ cup blanched almonds
3 tablespoons sugar
¼ cup powdered sugar
1 egg white, lightly beaten
30 dried apricot halves
15 pitted dates
2 teaspoons lime-flavored oil

1. In food processor, process pistachios, almonds and granulated sugar until finely ground.

2. Add powdered sugar and egg white; process about 15 seconds or until mixture is stiff. Add more powdered sugar if needed.

3. Sandwich 1 teaspoon of mixture between 2 apricot halves. Cut one slit into each date and stuff with 1 teaspoonful mixture. Repeat until all apricots, dates and filling are used. Before serving, brush with lime-flavored oil; sprinkle with reserved pistachios.

30 pieces

New Era
HANUKKAH

by Ethel G. Hofman

New Era
HANUKKAH

MENU

MEDITERRANEAN WHITE GAZPACHO

CHICKEN ROASTED WITH LEMON AND OLIVES

COLOSSAL PUMPKIN LATKE

CHUNKY ISRAELI SALAD

CHARRED RED AND YELLOW BELL PEPPERS

FRUIT COCKTAIL KUGEL

Serves 4

MENU SUGGESTIONS

Assorted Crispbreads

Lemon Ice

Fresh Strawberries and Pineapple

Hanukkah lasts for eight days. A full-blown home-cooked meal every night is time consuming and a lot of work. So for good taste, speed and diversity, try this menu which uses off-the-shelf convenience products and time-saving kitchen appliances. While traditional Hanukkah ingredients such as oils and dairy products are included, lengthy preparation and cooking are almost eliminated. Plus, this menu provides a "lighter" alternative to more traditional Hanukkah fare.

For widespread appeal, this menu is influenced by international flavors: Olive oil and olives from the Mediterranean; cilantro native to the East; ginger from tropical and sub-tropical areas like India and Jamaica; and oregano in the Greek and Italian dishes. All this and more packs each dish with freshness and tantalizing taste.

Once again — you don't have to be Jewish to try a Hanukkah celebration, or just try out this wonderful menu. It is easy to make no matter who you are or what you're celebrating!

New Era Hanukkah

Chicken Roasted with Lemon Olives

MEDITERRANEAN WHITE GAZPACHO

This creamy, garlic-flavored soup is dairy-free, so may be included in a meat or dairy meal. It is best served at room temperature.

8   slices white bread, ½ inch thick, crusts removed
¼   cup white vinegar
1   cup slivered blanched almonds
1   tablespoon minced garlic
2½   cups vegetable broth
½   cup olive oil
1   cup seedless green grapes
⅛   teaspoon salt
⅛   teaspoon freshly ground pepper

1. Pour about ¾ cup cold water over bread and let stand 5 minutes. Squeeze out as much liquid as possible.

2. Place bread in food processor with vinegar, almonds, garlic and 1 cup of the broth. Process until smooth and creamy. With motor running, gradually pour in olive oil.

3. Add grapes, salt and pepper; process to chop coarsely. Add remaining broth; process 30 seconds. (Mixture should be consistency of heavy cream. Add more broth if needed.) Garnish with grapes.

4 servings

CHICKEN ROASTED WITH LEMON AND OLIVES

This dish is influenced be commonly used Middle Eastern ingredients. Tangy lemon, oil-cured olives and fresh cilantro all blend together to infuse the chicken with sunny flavor. Do not substitute canned olives for oil-cured.

1   (3½-lb.) cut-up frying chicken
1   cup oil-cured olives, pitted
2   lemons, thinly sliced
2   tablespoons olive oil
¼   cup snipped cilantro
1   teaspoon lemon pepper seasoning
    Cilantro sprigs

1. Heat oven to 400°F. Insert three olives and two lemon slices under skin of each piece of chicken. Set aside.

2. Pour 1 tablespoon of the oil into baking dish. Add remaining olives, lemons and cilantro, spreading evenly over the bottom of dish. Arrange chicken pieces on top. Brush with remaining olive oil; sprinkle with lemon pepper seasoning.

3. Bake, uncovered, 15 minutes. Reduce heat to 375°F. Continue baking an additional 30 minutes or until internal temperature reaches 180°F. Garnish with cilantro sprigs.

4 servings

COLOSSAL PUMPKIN LATKE

Grate pumpkin on the smaller side of a grater. Try substituting winter squash for pumpkin. Serve with a fruit chutney.

1   (6-oz.) pkg. potato latke mix
2   eggs
1   cup cold water
¾   cup grated pumpkin
3   tablespoons cinnamon sugar*
2   teaspoons grated fresh ginger
      or ¾ teaspoon dried
      Vegetable oil

1. Prepare latke batter with eggs and water according to package directions. Stir in pumpkin, cinnamon sugar and ginger.

2. Heat about ⅛-inch oil in large skillet over medium-high heat. Spoon one-half of mixture into pan, spreading with the back of a wooden spoon to cover bottom of skillet. Reduce heat to medium. Cook 5 to 6 minutes or until firm and crisp on bottom. Turn with wide spatula; cook an additional 2 to 3 minutes or until brown. Turn out onto platter. Serve hot.

2 large latkes

* TIP

Cinnamon sugar is granulated sugar combined or scented with cinnamon.

MAKE-AHEAD CONVENIENCE

This menu is ideal for a Friday night (Shabbat) supper too—anytime you want to save work and still have a great meal. The items are quick and easy; and if desired, all the dishes may be made ahead. Flavors are enhanced by preparing the day or evening before.

- The Colossal Pumpkin Latke may be reheated to original crispness for 5 to 10 minutes in a 375°F oven.

- Using convenience items such as vegetable broth and garlic already minced in a jar, you can make Mediterranean White Gazpacho in minutes in your food processor.

- Chicken is traditional for Shabbat, and lemons and olives infuse their zest to brighten what could otherwise be a bland dish.

- Canned fruit cocktail and peach pie filling make short work of assembling Fruit Cocktail Kugel, which may be mixed, refrigerated and baked several days ahead, then refrigerated or frozen. If frozen, place in refrigerator the day before your event, and heat through at 350°F before serving.

Colossal Pumpkin Latke

Chunky Israeli Salad

CHUNKY ISRAELI SALAD

Israeli salad is distinguished by finely chopped tomatoes and cucumbers. This version contains similar ingredients, but to save time, try halved grape tomatoes and use scissors to snip parsley and mint. The refreshing dressing is bottled vinaigrette with fresh lemon juice and seasonings.

Dressing
- ¼ cup bottled oil and vinegar dressing
- 3 tablespoons lemon juice
- ¼ teaspoon garlic powder
- ⅛ teaspoon salt
- ⅛ teaspoon freshly ground pepper

Salad
- 1 cup yellow grape tomatoes, halved
- 1 cup red grape tomatoes, halved
- 3 cucumbers, unpeeled, diced ½-inch thick
- 1 rib celery, thinly sliced
- 1 scallion, thinly sliced
- ¼ cup coarsely snipped parsley
- ¼ cup finely shredded fresh mint

1. In small bowl, whisk together oil, lemon juice, garlic powder, salt and pepper. Set aside.

2. In large bowl, combine tomatoes, cucumbers, celery, scallion, parsley and mint. Pour dressing over salad; toss gently to mix. Serve chilled.

4 servings

CHARRED RED AND YELLOW BELL PEPPERS

Bell peppers now come in many colors. In season, bell peppers are cheap. Winter imports, especially the yellow and orange, are expensive so feel free to substitute as available. Broiling enhances the natural sweetness of the bell peppers but watch carefully to avoid scorching.

2 red bell peppers, seeded
2 yellow bell peppers, seeded
2 to 3 tablespoons olive oil
2 teaspoons dried oregano
2 tablespoons finely shredded
    fresh basil or 2 teaspoons dried
1 tablespoon kosher (coarse) salt

1. Heat broiler. Spray broiler pan with nonstick vegetable spray. Cut peppers into strips about ¾-inch wide and arrange on pan, cut sides down. Brush with olive oil; sprinkle with oregano, basil and salt. Drizzle with remaining oil.

2. Broil until skins begin to char. Turn heat off, cover loosely with aluminum foil and leave in oven an additional 5 minutes. Serve hot.

4 servings

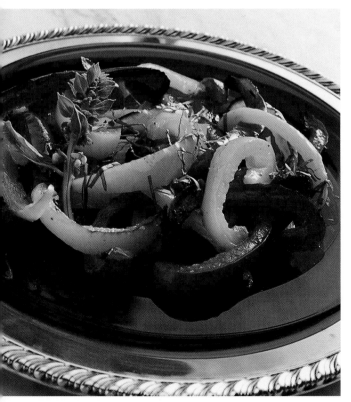

Charred Red and Yellow Bell Peppers

FRUIT COCKTAIL KUGEL

A favorite dish of Eastern European Jews, kugels are traditionally associated with holidays. Kugel is a cakelike pudding, usually made with dairy products and noodles. If desired, this recipe may be divided into two 9-inch square pans. Because this is a pareve dish, serve it as a meat, dairy or vegetarian meal.

8 oz. vermicelli, cooked, drained
2 tablespoons butter
¼ cup frozen orange juice concentrate
¼ cup sugar
¼ teaspoon salt
1 (8¾-oz.) can fruit cocktail, undrained
1 (21-oz.) can peach pie filling
¾ cup liquid nondairy creamer
3 eggs
2 tablespoons packed brown sugar
2 tablespoons ground almonds

1. Heat oven to 350°F. Spray 12 x 8-inch baking dish with nonstick cooking spray. In large bowl, combine hot, cooked noodles, butter, orange juice, sugar and salt. Stir in fruit cocktail and peach pie filling. Cool slightly.

2. Make a well in center. Whisk together eggs and creamer; fold into noodle mixture. Pour into baking dish. Combine brown sugar and almonds; sprinkle over top. Bake 50 to 60 minutes or until browned and crust is crisp. Cut into squares to serve warm or at room temperature.

About 15 servings

New Era Hanukkah

Holiday
COOKIES

by Nancy Baggett

Sharing and togetherness are a big part of the holiday season. So what could be more appropriate than gathering with friends and family to share recipes and swap favorite cookies?

A cookie exchange can be a fairly large, structured party, or a small and informal get-together. Some cookie exchanges feature up to a dozen or more guests, elaborate decorations and a potluck or other meal as part of the party. Others involve a small group of good friends meeting for coffee (or tea, mulled wine or cider) and conversation, and to casually sample and swap

continued on page 62

60

These are fragra
abundance of gol
walnuts. They ar
popular in Amer
Almost every hou
several rather diff
dropped from a s
out. Nearly all, h
and kept well. N
one colorful expla
do well when left

This recipe makes
snacking or gift-g

  1 cup dark r
  1 cup golder
1½ cups dried
 ¼ cup orange
 ¼ cup orange
  3 cups all-pu
  1 teaspoon c
  1 teaspoon n
  1 teaspoon b
 ¼ teaspoon s
  1 cup unsalte
  2 cups packe
  2 eggs
 ⅓ cup sour cr
  2 teaspoons
1½ cups chopp

1. In large, no
   marmalade
   combined.
   most moist

2. Heat oven
   nonstick co
   flour, cinna
   until well b

Holiday
COOKIES

LEMON-TANGERINE DAINTIES

HOLIDAY HERMITS

CHRISTMAS VANILLA
ICEBOX SLICES

DOUBLE ALMOND DREAMS

CHOCOLATE-GLAZED
HONEY-NUT FINGERS

CRANBERRY-SPICE BISCOTTI
WITH WHITE CHOCOLATE

FOUR-SPICE CRACKLES

CHERRY-RASPBERRY
CINNAMON STREUSEL BARS

CITRUS-SPICE SUGAR COOKIES

APRICOT-PISTACHIO
THUMBPRINTS

CHOCOLATE CHIP MERINGUES

Christmas Vanilla Icebox Slices

their favorite

old-fashione

several cooks

up their coll

of cookie ex

spacious, we

In every cas

exhangers er

they just bal

No matter

even if you

yourself, far

ideas that fo

LEMO
DAIN

Individually

in this case,

simply dipp

shaken off.

appearance,

cookie tray

Be sure to k

well as their

Cookies

3 cups

I teasp

⅛ teasp

½ teasp

1¼ cups

I cup s

COORDINATING A
COOKIE EXCHANGE

Whatever kind of cookie exchange you choose, planning and coordination are a must. Invite guests well ahead, as the holidays are busy and calendars fill up. Even with advance notice, not everyone will be available, and there will likely be cancellations, so keep this in mind when deciding how many people to invite.

It's also important to give guests guidance on what's expected. For example, if you'd like participants to share their recipes, be sure to tell them how many copies they'll need for the group. And it's always wise to tactfully stress that the cookies should be "from scratch" and that festive, seasonal varieties are particularly

continued on page 66

CHRISTMAS VANILLA
ICEBOX SLICES

Like most icebox cookie recipes, these feature convenient logs of dough that are chilled, then cut crosswise into slices and baked as needed. However, these slices have a wonderful sandy-crisp texture and festive appearance that take them beyond the ordinary. They are an especially good choice when you need a large batch for holiday entertaining, gift giving or participating in a cookie exchange, but are short on time or want to do much of the preparation ahead.

One secret to the pleasing appearance is in applying alternating lines of red and green crystal sugar along the lengths of the logs prior to slicing. The decorating technique is quite easy; just follow the directions given in the recipe. The dough slices neatly and forms evenly-shaped finished cookies.

2¾ cups all-purpose flour
¼ cup cornstarch
¾ teaspoon baking powder
¼ teaspoon baking soda
I cup unsalted butter, slightly softened
6 tablespoons canola oil
1¼ cups powdered sugar
¼ cup sugar
I egg
½ teaspoon salt
2½ teaspoons vanilla
¼ cup each red and green coarse crystal sugar

1. In large bowl, stir together flour, cornstarch, baking powder and baking soda. In large bowl, beat butter, oil, powdered sugar and sugar at medium speed until lightened and fluffy. Beat in egg, salt and vanilla until very well blended and smooth. Beat or stir flour mixture into butter mixture until well blended. Let stand about 5 minutes, until the dough firms up slightly.

2. Divide dough in half. Place each portion on a 15-inch sheet of parchment paper. With greased hands, pat and smooth each portion into a rough log about 11-inches long. Roll paper around each log, smoothing and pressing out middle until evenly thick and well-shaped, about 12 inches long. Twist

paper ends to prevent it from unrolling. Freeze logs on tray or baking sheet at least 3 hours or up to 24 hours,* or until dough is very cold and firm.

3. Heat oven to 350°F. Spray several baking sheets with nonstick cooking spray. Peel paper off frozen dough. Sprinkle 15-inch-long sheet of parchment paper with 12 x ¼-inch line of red sugar; use long-bladed spatula, dull edge of a long knife or ruler to scrape sugar into an evenly-thick, ¼-inch line. Repeat with a second parchment paper sheet and green sugar.

4. Press length of log into line of red sugar until a tidy line of sugar is imbedded along length of dough. Rotate log one-quarter turn, then press into green sugar to form a green line along length of log. Refresh and tidy lines of colored sugar on papers, then repeat imbedding process by rotating a quarter turn, adding another red line, then rotating another quarter turn and adding a green line. Repeat entire decorating process with second log. If dough is very hard, let it stand on cutting board a few minutes, but don't oversoften; it should be soft enough to cut without cracking and breaking apart, but firm enough to slice neatly.

5. Using large sharp knife and working on a cutting board, cut logs into ¼-inch slices. Wipe knife clean between cuts, as necessary. Using spatula, immediately transfer slices to baking sheets, spacing about 2 inches apart. Put a pinch of additional green or red sugar on center tops of cookies, if desired.

6. Bake cookies in upper third of oven 5 to 8 minutes, or until edges are dark. Rotate pan halfway through baking to ensure even browning. Remove pan from oven; let cookies firm up 1 or 2 minutes. Using a wide spatula, gently transfer cookies to wire racks. Let stand until completely cooled. Store cookies in airtight container 2 to 3 weeks, or freeze up to 2 months.

About 6 dozen cookies

* TIP

The dough may be decorated, sliced and baked immediately, or wrapped neatly in plastic wrap, placed in a plastic bag and returned to freezer up to one month.

DOUBLE ALMOND DREAMS

Double almond dreams have a deep, full almond flavor and fragrance due to the addition of both almond paste and almond extract. Chopped almonds also provide a nice crunch in the tender, buttery dough.

These cheerful, cherry-decorated rounds are perfect not only for serving and gift-giving, but for sharing at a cookie exchange.

2 egg yolks
1 (7- to 8-oz.) pkg. or can almond paste,
    cut into small pieces
1 cup sugar
1¾ cups unsalted butter, slightly softened
2 teaspoons vanilla
1 teaspoon almond extract
½ teaspoon salt
¼ teaspoon baking powder
3½ cups all-purpose flour
1 cup plus 3 tablespoons chopped blanched almonds,
    About 20 candied cherries, quartered

1. Heat oven to 375°F. Spray several baking sheets with nonstick cooking spray.

2. In large bowl beat egg yolks, almond paste and sugar at medium speed about 3 minutes or until almond paste is thoroughly incorporated. Add butter; continue beating until very fluffy and smooth. Thoroughly beat in vanilla, almond extract, salt and baking powder. Gradually beat in flour until thoroughly incorporated but not overmixed; if mixer motor labors, stir in remaining flour using a large wooden spoon. Fold in 1 cup almonds with spoon.

3. Shape dough into 1-inch balls. Space cookies about 2½ inches apart on baking sheet; don't crowd as dough will spread. Press balls down using palm until circles are about 1½ inches in diameter. Sprinkle a few chopped almonds over each cookie, pressing almonds lightly into dough. Press 1 cherry quarter into center of each cookie.

4. Bake cookies in middle third of oven 8 to 11 minutes or until just slightly colored on top and barely brown at edges. Remove from oven; let cookies stand 3 to 4 minutes, then carefully transfer to wire racks. Let stand until thoroughly cooled. Store in airtight container up to 10 days. Freeze up to one month.

About 7 dozen cookies

CHOCOLATE-GLAZED HONEY-NUT FINGERS

These chewy, nut-and-honey-flavored bars disappear fast from a holiday cookie tray and also make an appealing, eagerly received homemade gift or cookie exchange selection. If you need a larger quantity, the recipe can be doubled. To double, bake the bars in 2 (13x9-inch) pans or in 1 (12x18x1-inch) pan.

1	cup unsalted butter, slightly softened
½	cup sugar
1	egg
1½	cups all-purpose flour
¼	teaspoon baking powder
¼	teaspoon salt
⅔	cup mild honey
¼	cup packed brown sugar
¼	teaspoon salt
1¼	cups chopped almonds
1	cup chopped walnuts
2	teaspoons vanilla
1	cup semisweet chocolate chips

1. Heat oven to 400°F. Line baking sheet with heavy-duty aluminum foil, allowing foil to overhang two narrow ends by about 2 inches.

2. Beat together ½ cup of the butter, sugar and egg at medium speed about 2 minutes or until light and fluffy. In small deep bowl, thoroughly stir together flour, baking powder and ¼ teaspoon salt. Beat or stir flour mixture into butter mixture until well blended and smooth. Turn out dough into pan. Using greased hands, press dough firmly into pan. Lay one sheet of parchment paper over dough. Continue pressing down and smoothing out to edges to form smooth, even layer. Carefully peel off paper. Prick dough all over with fork.

3. Bake on middle oven rack 11 to 15 minutes or until cookies are lightly browned all over and slightly darker at edges. Set aside.

4. For honey-nut layer, heat oven to 350°F. In medium saucepan, melt remaining butter over medium-high heat. Using long-handled wooden spoon, stir in honey, brown sugar, salt and 2 cups of the almonds and walnuts (reserve remaining ¼ cup nuts for garnish). Bring mixture to a boil over medium-high heat. When it comes to a full boil, adjust heat so mixture boils briskly; cook for exactly 3½ minutes, stirring occasionally, being careful not to splash hot liquid. Remove from heat; stir in vanilla.

5. Pour mixture over dough in pan, spreading evenly to edges. Bake on upper oven rack 9 to 13 minutes or until top is deep golden brown and bubbly all over. Remove from oven; let cool on wire rack 30 minutes. Sprinkle chocolate chips evenly over top. When chocolate melts, spread evenly over bars. Sprinkle remaining ¼ cup nuts evenly over top.

6. Refrigerate at least 1 hour until cold and firm. Lift foil and bars from pan. Carefully peel off foil. Transfer slab to cutting board. Trim away and discard overbaked edges all around. To form fingers, mark and cut slab crosswise into fifths and lengthwise into eighths. Retrace cuts to separate pieces, if necessary. Fingers will keep, in airtight container, up to 2 weeks. Wrapped airtight, they may be frozen up to 2 months.

About 3½ dozen bars

continued from page 64

welcome. (You might offer to provide some of your own never-fail recipes to cooks who seem uncertain about what to make.)

Of course, the most important information to convey is how many cookies participants should bring. For a small group, you might ask each person to bring enough to swap a dozen with everyone else attending. This is impractical for a group much larger than six, however, because few cooks these days have time to make hundreds of cookies, even if it's all one kind. A sensible solution is to suggest that everyone bring six dozen, plus a few extra for on-site sampling. Then, if there are six participants, they take home 12 of every other participant's cookies; if there are eight participants; they take home 9 of each sort; if there are 12, they get six of each variety; and so on.

While it isn't obligatory, it's nice to supply cookie take-home containers for your guests. (Otherwise, be sure to remind them to bring their own.) Suitable inexpensive yet festive-looking options include sturdy decorative

continued on page 69

CRANBERRY-SPICE BISCOTTI WITH WHITE CHOCOLATE

Crystallized ginger, coriander and cardamom bring out the flavor of the dried cranberries, and white chocolate adds a complimentary mellowness.

Biscotti
1¾ cups dried cranberries
⅓ cup chopped crystallized ginger
3⅓ cups all-purpose flour
2½ teaspoons baking powder
1¼ teaspoons ground coriander
½ teaspoon ground cardamom
¼ teaspoon salt
1 cup sugar
⅓ cup unsalted butter, slightly softened
1 tablespoon finely grated fresh lemon peel
2 eggs
2 tablespoons lemon juice
4 teaspoons light corn syrup
2½ teaspoons vanilla

Glaze
8 oz. white chocolate, coarsely chopped
4 teaspoons shortening

1. Heat oven to 350°F. Line several baking sheets with parchment paper. Place cranberries and ginger in food processor; process until finely chopped.

2. In medium bowl, combine flour, baking powder, coriander, cardamom and salt; mix well. In large bowl, beat sugar, butter and lemon peel at medium speed until light, fluffy and well blended. Add eggs, lemon juice, corn syrup and vanilla; beat until blended (mixture may look curdled).

3. Gradually beat one-half of flour mixture into egg mixture just until well blended. Beat in remaining flour mixture until blended. Stir in cranberry mixture until evenly distributed.

4. Divide dough in half. Roll one-half on large sheet of plastic wrap; shape into 15x1¾-inch log. Remove plastic wrap and place on baking sheet; repeat with remaining half of dough, arranging logs as far apart as possible on baking sheet. Press down logs to ¾-inch thickness.

5. Bake 30 to 35 minutes or until well browned and slightly cracked. Place parchment paper and logs on wire rack; cool 20 to 30 minutes. Keep oven at 350°F.

6. Line 2 baking sheets with parchment paper. Transfer logs to cutting board. With serrated knife, cut diagonally into scant ½-inch-thick slices. Lay slices cut side down on baking sheets. Return to oven; bake 16 minutes or until lightly browned, turning once. Remove from baking sheets; cool on wire racks.

7. Line 2 baking sheets with aluminum foil. In large, shallow microwave-safe bowl, combine white chocolate and shortening; microwave on medium 2½ to 3½ minutes, stopping and stirring every 30 seconds until chocolate is almost melted. Stir until chocolate is completely melted.

8. Dip top edge of each biscotti in melted chocolate; place on baking sheets. Let stand 10 to 20 minutes, or until chocolate is set. Store cookies in airtight container at room temperature up to 3 weeks.

About 4 dozen cookies

Cranberry-Spice Biscotti with White Chocolate

FOUR-SPICE CRACKLES

Prepared with a bold, enticing four-spice blend, these cookies will perfume the whole house with their distinctive gingerbread scent. Crackles get their name from dramatic-looking surface cracks that develop as they bake.

2½ cups all-purpose flour
 1 teaspoon baking powder
 ½ teaspoon baking soda
 ¼ teaspoon salt
1½ teaspoons ground ginger
 1 teaspoon ground cloves
 1 teaspoon nutmeg
 ¾ teaspoon cinnamon
 1 cup packed brown sugar
 ½ cup unsalted butter, softened
 ½ cup shortening
 ¼ cup molasses
 1 egg
    About ⅔ cup coarse sugar*

1. In large bowl, combine flour, baking powder, baking soda, salt, ginger, cloves, nutmeg and cinnamon; mix well. Set aside. In another large bowl, beat brown sugar, butter, shortening and molasses at medium speed about 2 minutes or until well blended and fluffy. Add egg; beat until well blended and smooth.

2. Add one-half of flour mixture to butter mixture; beat until well blended. Beat in remaining flour mixture just until blended. Cover dough and refrigerate 1½ hours or until firm enough to shape into balls. (Dough can be refrigerated up to 24 hours.)

3. Place oven rack in upper third of oven; heat oven to 375°F. Line several baking sheets with parchment paper. With lightly greased hands, roll dough into 1-inch balls. Roll balls in coarse sugar; place about 2½ inches apart on baking sheets.

4. Bake 9 to 12 minutes or until cookies are cracked and slightly soft in center. Remove from baking sheet; cool on wire racks. Store cookies in airtight container up to 2 weeks; freeze up to 1 month.

About 4½ dozen cookies

✲ TIP

If you can't find coarse sugar, substitute regular sugar.

CHERRY-RASPBERRY CINNAMON STREUSEL BARS

A crispy-crunchy streusel topping and zesty filling make these bars a great addition to your holiday cookie tray!

Filling
1½ cups dried cherries
1 cup raspberry preserves
5 tablespoons kirsch or water
½ teaspoon cinnamon

Streusel
1½ cups all-purpose flour
1 cup old-fashioned, quick-cooking oats
1 cup sugar
1 tablespoon cinnamon
½ teaspoon nutmeg
¼ teaspoon salt
⅔ cup unsalted butter, melted
1 teaspoon almond extract
1 cup sliced almonds

Icing
1 cup powdered sugar
3 to 4 teaspoons milk

1. Heat oven to 350°F. Spray 13 x 9-inch pan with nonstick cooking spray.

2. In medium saucepan, combine cherries, preserves, 3 tablespoons of the kirsch and ½ teaspoon cinnamon. Bring to a boil over medium-high heat. Cook and stir 3 to 4 minutes or until cherries soften slightly. (Mixture will be runny.) Transfer mixture to food processor; pulse until mixture is just coarsely pureed. Set aside.

3. In large bowl, combine flour, oats, sugar, 1 tablespoon cinnamon, nutmeg and salt; mix well. Add butter and almond extract; stir until mixture is well blended and crumbly. Firmly press one-half of mixture evenly in bottom of pan. (Reserve remaining struesel mixture for topping.)

4. Bake 12 minutes. Evenly spread filling over baked layer.

continued from page 66

paper plates and plastic wrap to cover, or cellophane bags and wired ribbon for twist ties.

Remember to supply at least several containers per guest. That way, spicy cookies can be kept separate from mild butter and sugar cookies (otherwise the mild ones will take on a spice taste); and crispy, dry cookies are separated from soft, gooey ones (otherwise the crisp ones will go limp). Store any powdered sugar-coated or tender cookies by themselves.

With the details taken care of, all the ingredients for a happy holiday are in place: good friends, a sharing spirit, a little time for mingling, and of course, great cookies!

5. Add almonds and remaining kirsch to remaining streusel mixture; mix until streusel is lightly moistened. Spread streusel evenly over filling, breaking up any large clumps with fingertips; pat down lightly.

6. Bake 20 to 25 minutes or until streusel topping is lightly browned. Cool in pan on wire rack.

7. Meanwhile, in small bowl, combine sugar and milk; blend well. Drizzle over cooled bars. Let stand until set. Cut bars into 24 squares; cut each square diagonally in half to form 48 bars. Bars can be made up to 1 week ahead. Store in airtight container.

4 dozen bars

Cherry-Raspberry Cinnamon Steusel Bars

APRICOT-PISTACHIO THUMBPRINTS

Fragrant and festive, these handsome cookies feature an unusual blend of coriander, allspice and ginger. This spice combination is a perfect complement to the apricot preserves and pistachio nuts.

2½ cups all-purpose flour
 2 teaspoons ground coriander
 ¾ teaspoon ground ginger
 ¾ teaspoon ground allspice
 ½ teaspoon baking soda
 ¼ teaspoon salt
 1 cup unsalted butter, softened
 ¾ cup sugar
 1 egg
1¼ cups apricot preserves
 ½ teaspoon almond extract
 ½ teaspoon lemon extract
 1 teaspoon finely grated fresh orange peel
 1 cup finely chopped pistachios

1. Heat oven to 350°F. Line several baking sheets with parchment paper. In medium bowl, combine flour, coriander, ginger, allspice, baking soda and salt; mix well. Set aside.

2. In large bowl, beat butter at medium speed until light and smooth. Add sugar and egg; beat until fluffy and well blended. Add ¼ cup of the apricot preserves, almond extract, lemon extract and orange peel; beat until combined. Reduce speed to low. Add one-half of the flour mixture; beat just until combined. Beat in remaining flour mixture and ⅓ cup of the pistachios until thoroughly blended. Cover; refrigerate dough 45 minutes or until chilled.

CHERRY-RASPBERRY CINNAMON STREUSEL BARS

A crispy-crunchy streusel topping and zesty filling make these bars a great addition to your holiday cookie tray!

Filling
1½ cups dried cherries
1 cup raspberry preserves
5 tablespoons kirsch or water
½ teaspoon cinnamon

Streusel
1½ cups all-purpose flour
1 cup old-fashioned, quick-cooking oats
1 cup sugar
1 tablespoon cinnamon
½ teaspoon nutmeg
¼ teaspoon salt
⅔ cup unsalted butter, melted
1 teaspoon almond extract
1 cup sliced almonds

Icing
1 cup powdered sugar
3 to 4 teaspoons milk

1. Heat oven to 350°F. Spray 13x9-inch pan with nonstick cooking spray.

2. In medium saucepan, combine cherries, preserves, 3 tablespoons of the kirsch and ½ teaspoon cinnamon. Bring to a boil over medium-high heat. Cook and stir 3 to 4 minutes or until cherries soften slightly. (Mixture will be runny.) Transfer mixture to food processor; pulse until mixture is just coarsely pureed. Set aside.

3. In large bowl, combine flour, oats, sugar, 1 tablespoon cinnamon, nutmeg and salt; mix well. Add butter and almond extract; stir until mixture is well blended and crumbly. Firmly press one-half of mixture evenly in bottom of pan. (Reserve remaining struesel mixture for topping.)

4. Bake 12 minutes. Evenly spread filling over baked layer.

continued from page 66

paper plates and plastic wrap to cover, or cellophane bags and wired ribbon for twist ties.

Remember to supply at least several containers per guest. That way, spicy cookies can be kept separate from mild butter and sugar cookies (otherwise the mild ones will take on a spice taste); and crispy, dry cookies are separated from soft, gooey ones (otherwise the crisp ones will go limp). Store any powdered sugar-coated or tender cookies by themselves.

With the details taken care of, all the ingredients for a happy holiday are in place: good friends, a sharing spirit, a little time for mingling, and of course, great cookies!

5. Add almonds and remaining kirsch to remaining streusel mixture; mix until streusel is lightly moistened. Spread streusel evenly over filling, breaking up any large clumps with fingertips; pat down lightly.

6. Bake 20 to 25 minutes or until streusel topping is lightly browned. Cool in pan on wire rack.

7. Meanwhile, in small bowl, combine sugar and milk; blend well. Drizzle over cooled bars. Let stand until set. Cut bars into 24 squares; cut each square diagonally in half to form 48 bars. Bars can be made up to 1 week ahead. Store in airtight container.

4 dozen bars

Cherry-Raspberry Cinnamon Steusel Bars

Holiday Cookies

Citrus-Spice Sugar Cookies

These cookies are a spicy change of pace from ordinary sugar cookies. Lemon, orange and spices combine to give the crispy cutouts delicate flavor. Rolling the dough between parchment paper makes it easy to roll and cut out cookies using this delicate dough; it also makes for easier cleanup.

CITRUS-SPICE SUGAR COOKIES

Cookies

2	cups all-purpose flour
1	teaspoon ground ginger
½	teaspoon baking powder
½	teaspoon five-spice powder
¼	teaspoon salt
¼	teaspoon allspice
1	cup sugar
¾	cup unsalted butter, slightly softened
1½	teaspoons finely grated fresh orange peel
1	teaspoon finely grated fresh lemon peel
2	tablespoons light corn syrup
1½	teaspoons vanilla
2	egg yolks

Citrus Icing

1⅓	cups powdered sugar
½	teaspoon finely grated fresh orange peel
1	tablespoon orange juice
1	tablespoon lemon juice

1. In large bowl, combine flour, ginger, baking powder, five-spice powder, salt and allspice; mix well. Set aside.

2. In another large bowl beat sugar, butter, 1½ teaspoons orange peel and lemon peel at medium speed until light and well blended. Add corn syrup, vanilla and egg yolks; beat until mixed. Reduce speed to low; add flour mixture. Beat until well blended.

3. Divide dough in half. Place each portion between large sheets of parchment paper; roll out each to ⅛-inch thickness, occasionally checking underside of dough and smoothing out any wrinkles that form. Stack rolled portions (paper still attached) on baking sheet. Refrigerate about 30 minutes or until cold and firm. (Or freeze about 15 minutes to speed up chilling.)

4. Place oven rack in upper third of oven; heat oven to 375°F. Line several baking sheets with parchment paper. Working with one portion of dough at a time (keep remaining dough in refrigerator), gently peel away 1 sheet parchment paper, then replace with fresh sheet of parchment paper. (This will make it easier to lift cookies from paper later.) Invert dough; peel off and discard second layer of parchment paper. With 2½ to 3-inch assorted cutters, cut out cookies. With spatula, carefully transfer cookies from paper to baking sheets, placing about 2 inches apart.

5. Bake on upper oven rack 6 to 9 minutes or until edges are light brown. Cool on baking sheet 1 minute. Place cookies on wire rack; cool completely.

6. To prepare icing, in small bowl, combine sugar, orange peel, orange juice and lemon juice; beat at medium speed until smooth. If necessary, add additional orange juice or water until of piping or drizzling consistency. Decorate cookies as desired. Let stand until icing is completely set, at least 1 hour. Store cookies in airtight container up to 2 weeks.

About 4 dozen cookies

Apricot-Pistachio Thumbprints

APRICOT-PISTACHIO THUMBPRINTS

Fragrant and festive, these handsome cookies feature an unusual blend of coriander, allspice and ginger. This spice combination is a perfect complement to the apricot preserves and pistachio nuts.

2½ cups all-purpose flour
 2 teaspoons ground coriander
 ¾ teaspoon ground ginger
 ¾ teaspoon ground allspice
 ½ teaspoon baking soda
 ¼ teaspoon salt
 1 cup unsalted butter, softened
 ¾ cup sugar
 1 egg
1¼ cups apricot preserves
 ½ teaspoon almond extract
 ½ teaspoon lemon extract
 1 teaspoon finely grated fresh orange peel
 1 cup finely chopped pistachios

1. Heat oven to 350°F. Line several baking sheets with parchment paper. In medium bowl, combine flour, coriander, ginger, allspice, baking soda and salt; mix well. Set aside.

2. In large bowl, beat butter at medium speed until light and smooth. Add sugar and egg; beat until fluffy and well blended. Add ¼ cup of the apricot preserves, almond extract, lemon extract and orange peel; beat until combined. Reduce speed to low. Add one-half of the flour mixture; beat just until combined. Beat in remaining flour mixture and ⅓ cup of the pistachios until thoroughly blended. Cover; refrigerate dough 45 minutes or until chilled.

72

3. Place remaining ⅔ cup pistachios in small bowl. Roll dough into 1-inch balls. Roll balls in pistachios until coated; place 1½ inches apart on baking sheets. With thumb, make a deep indentation in center of each ball.

4. Bake 9 to 12 minutes or until cookies are light brown. Remove from oven; cool on baking sheet 1 minute. Place cookies on wire racks; cool completely.

5. Press center of cookies again to form deep indentations. Fill with remaining 1 cup apricot preserves. Store cookies in airtight container up to 10 days; freeze up to 1 month.

About 5 dozen cookies

CHOCOLATE CHIP MERINGUES

These cookies feature pleasing chewy-soft centers and great chocolate aroma. Be sure to bake all the cookies at once; one pan of cookies may deflate somewhat if allowed to stand while the other bakes.

¾   cup powdered sugar
4   teaspoons unsweetened Dutch-process cocoa
1   teaspoon cinnamon
4   egg whites
½   cup sugar
1   teaspoon vanilla
¼   cup plus 3 tablespoons miniature semisweet
       chocolate chips
1½   teaspoons shortening

1. Place 2 oven racks, one above the other, in center third of oven; heat oven to 275°F. Line two baking sheets with parchment paper. In small bowl, combine powdered sugar, cocoa and cinnamon; mix well. Set aside.

2. In large bowl, beat egg whites at low speed until foamy. Gradually increase speed to medium-high; beat until stiff peaks just begin to form. While mixer is running, pour sugar in steady stream into egg whites. Continue beating until mixture stands in stiff peaks. Beat in vanilla until well blended.

3. Sift powdered sugar mixture over meringue. With rubber scraper, gently fold mixture into meringue until partially incorporated. Sprinkle ¼ cup of the chips over meringue and continue folding just until evenly incorporated. Do not overmix as meringue may begin to deflate.

4. Spoon heaping teaspoons of meringue into peaked mounds about 1¾ inches in diameter on baking sheets. (A pastry bag may also be used.)

5. Place baking sheets on separate racks in center of oven; bake 15 minutes. Switch positions of baking sheets in oven; bake an additional 17 to 20 minutes or until cookies are dry to the touch, but still slightly soft in center when pressed. With cookies still attached to paper, place on flat surface until completely cooled.

6. To prepare chocolate glaze, in small microwave-safe bowl, combine remaining 3 tablespoons chips and shortening. Microwave on high 1 minute. Stir well; microwave on medium, stopping and stirring at 30 second intervals, until chips and shortening are just melted and smooth.

7. Spoon chocolate glaze into small pastry bag fitted with fine tip, or small resealable plastic bag with small hole cut in one bottom corner. Drizzle fine lines of chocolate back and forth over cookie tops. Let cookies stand in cool place until chocolate sets. Store cookies in airtight container in single layer in cool, dry place.

About 3½ dozen cookies

Outdoor Activity

PARTY

by Mary Evans

No matter where you live, Christmastime is colder than the rest of the year. Of course just how cold it gets is a relative thing, but the end result is the same: We often coop ourselves up indoors. What a shame! There are so many great winter outdoor activities to partake in…if the fresh air and fun aren't enough to get you out there, maybe the reward of this delicious menu waiting indoors will spur you into action.

Outdoor Activity

PARTY

MENU

VENISON CHILI

JALAPENO CHEESE
AND CORNMEAL BREAD

HOT BUTTERED CIDER

MEXICAN CHOCOLATE
PUDDING CAKE

Serves 8

To have this menu ready for guests after caroling, sledding, skating, cross-country skiing, hiking or any other winter outdoor activity, put the hot buttered cider in insulated beverage servers in advance. Heat the chili and slice the bread to serve. Pull the batter for the pudding cake from the refrigerator to complete and bake while enjoying your chili, then serve the dessert piping hot.

VENISON CHILI

3 tablespoons vegetable oil
2 lb. venison, cut into 1-inch cubes
2 large onions, chopped
1 tablespoon minced garlic
1 (28-oz.) can diced tomatoes, undrained
2 (14½-oz.) cans beef broth
1 (15-oz.) can pinto beans, rinsed, drained
1 (7-oz.) can diced green chiles
3 tablespoons chili powder
1½ teaspoons ground cumin
1½ teaspoons dried oregano, crushed
¼ teaspoon cinnamon
⅛ teaspoon cayenne
1 tablespoon honey
¼ cup cornmeal

1. In large saucepan, heat 2 tablespoons of the oil over medium-high heat until hot. Add venison in batches; brown on all sides, about 5 to 8 minutes per batch, removing to bowl when browned.

2. Add remaining 1 tablespoon oil to saucepan. Stir in onions; reduce heat to medium. Sauté about 5 to 8 minutes or until tender. Add garlic; sauté about 30 seconds to 1 minute or until fragrant.

3. Return venison to pan. Add tomatoes, broth, beans, chiles, chili powder, cumin, oregano, cinnamon, cayenne and honey; stir to combine. Push ingredients slightly to side; whisk cornmeal into liquid. Stir to combine. Bring to a boil; reduce heat to low and simmer, partially covered, 1 hour.

8 servings

GUIDE TO VENISON

The dark red meat of venison has a sweet, rich flavor. Its texture is similar to beef, but it is much leaner. Venison is wonderful in chili: The meat has a little more "whang" than beef, and the slow, moist cooking method adds moisture.

JALAPENO CHEESE AND CORNMEAL BREAD

This bread slices well and makes wonderful sandwiches. The cheese melts into the bread, leaving a surprising richness and heat.

¾ cup lukewarm water (105-110°F)
2 tablespoons sugar
1 (¼-oz.) pkg. dry yeast
2 tablespoons vegetable oil
1 egg
3 cups bread flour
1 cup shredded jalapeño-jack cheese
¼ cup yellow cornmeal
2 teaspoons salt

1. In medium bowl, stir together water, sugar and yeast. Let rest 5 minutes. Stir in oil and egg. In large bowl, stir together 2½ cups of the flour, cheese, cornmeal and salt. Stir in yeast mixture until mixture forms soft dough. Sprinkle remaining ½ cup flour on counter; turn out dough onto floured surface. Knead about 10 minutes or until smooth and elastic, working in flour on counter only as necessary to prevent sticking. Place in clean, lightly greased bowl; let rise 1 to 1½ hours or until doubled in bulk. Punch down; turn out onto lightly floured surface.

2. Spray baking sheet with nonstick cooking spray; dust with enough cornmeal to cover. Pat dough into an 8x14-inch rectangle. Roll up tightly starting at long side of dough. Pinch bottom and sides to seal. Place on baking sheet. Let rise about 45 minutes or until doubled in bulk.

3. Heat oven to 400°F. Bake 20 to 25 minutes or until loaf is dark brown and bottom sounds hollow when tapped. Cool on wire rack.

1 loaf

Venision Chili and Jalapeño Cheese and Cornmeal Bread

Hearty Venison Chili can be made ahead and reheated. Feel free to substitute pork or beef for the venison. Simmer until meat is tender, adding a bit of water if necessary as the chili thickens. Serve with your favorite condiments, such as sour cream, fresh cilantro leaves, chopped green onion or avocado.

Outdoor Activity Party

Mexican Chocolate Pudding Cake

HOT BUTTERED CIDER

This hot beverage is perfect for chilly winter evenings. For children or guests who avoid alcohol, omit the rum and butter.

  2 quarts apple cider
  8 sticks cinnamon
  8 whole cloves
  8 allspice berries
  3 (quarter-sized) slices peeled fresh ginger
  4 slices lemon, halved
 ¼ cup sugar
 ¾ cup dark rum
  8 teaspoons butter

1. In Dutch oven or large pot, heat cider, cinnamon, cloves, allspice berries, ginger, lemon and sugar over medium heat about 10 minutes or until boiling. Reduce heat to low; simmer 10 minutes to develop flavors. Strain, reserving lemon slices and cinnamon sticks. Cover and refrigerate, if desired; reheat before serving.

2. Measure 3 tablespoons rum into each of 8 (12-ounce) mugs. Ladle 1 cup hot cider into each mug, including cinnamon stick and lemon slice half if desired. Float 1 teaspoon pat of butter on surface of each mug.

8 servings

MEXICAN CHOCOLATE PUDDING CAKE

Mexican chocolate is often flavored with cinnamon and almonds. If desired, omit liqueur and increase the milk to ½ cup. Stir 1 teaspoon instant espresso powder into the milk for a rich coffee flavor.

  1 cup all-purpose flour
1¾ cups sugar
 ⅔ cup unsweetened Dutch-process cocoa
 ⅓ cup slivered almonds
  2 teaspoons ground cinnamon
 ¾ teaspoon baking powder
 ¾ teaspoon salt
  2 eggs
  6 tablespoons milk
  2 tablespoons coffee-flavored liqueur
  1 teaspoon vanilla
1⅓ cups boiling coffee
  1 quart vanilla ice cream

1. Heat oven to 350°F. In large bowl, combine flour, 1 cup of the sugar, ⅓ cup of the cocoa, almonds, cinnamon, baking powder and salt. In medium bowl, combine remaining sugar and cocoa; set aside.

2. In another medium bowl, whisk together eggs, milk, liqueur and vanilla. Pour into flour mixture and stir just until combined. Spread into 8-inch square pan. Batter can be prepared up to several hours ahead. Cover and refrigerate at this point.

3. Stir boiling coffee into sugar and cocoa mixture. Pour over batter in baking pan. Bake 30 to 35 minutes or until toothpick inserted in center comes out clean. Serve immediately with ice cream.

8 servings

Festive

Tamale Party

by Lisa Golden Schroeder

Festive
TAMALE PARTY

MENU

PICADILLO TAMALES

SALSA VERDE

TAOS SUPPER SALAD

FROZEN MARGARITA MOUSSES
WITH STRAWBERRY-MANGO SAUCE

Serves 6

In the desert Southwest, winter holidays may not resemble a snowy wonderland (unless you're high in the mountains of New Mexico or Arizona), but traditions are steadfast. Many families join together in December to make tamales at "tamalada parties."

Making tamales is a time-consuming process. But by taking advantage of sharing hands, an assembly line is created, cutting down on the time and work for any one person. The end result is worth the effort. It's a time for fun and togetherness—it's been said that "gossip is an essential ingredient" for a tamalada party.

Don't let the list of food ingredients deter you from making tamales; most of them are seasonings. The masa dough, made from fine corn flour (masa harina), is quite simple to prepare, then it's just spread onto dried corn husks that have been soaked in water. At

Christmas time, well-spiced savory fillings are most traditional, such as the recipe here that includes pork and beef. But tamales can change with the seasons, being made with "green corn" (dough made with fresh corn kernels) in the summer, or even dulce (sweet). Tamales dulce are served for dessert or snacks, with the masa sweetened and even tinted bright colors. Pumpkin, spices and dried or fresh fruit can all figure into the fillings or dough of sweet tamales.

Maybe it's time to start a new holiday tradition with family or friends. The Southwestern tastes and ideas in this tamale party could be just what you've been looking for!

Festive Tamale Party

Picadillo Tamales

PICADILLO TAMALES

Masa, the corn dough used for tortillas and tamales, is made from masa harina, a dehydrated yellow corn flour made from dried corn kernels that have been softened in a lime solution, then finely ground. Regular cornmeal, which is more coarsely ground, is not a good substitute. Masa harina is generally available in the baking section of the grocery with other flours. The more unusual blue cornmeal masa is available in New Mexico. Lard is the traditional fat used to make masa dough; it imparts a distinct flavor that can't be easily replaced. Masa must be vigorously beaten with a wooden spoon (or use an electric mixer) and should be so light that a spoonful can float on water. Toast and grind your own coriander and cumin seeds for a more pronounced depth of flavor. This picadillo-style filling is of Spanish origin, with some fruit that contributes slightly sweet overtones. Look for dried corn husks in the produce section of Latin American markets.

Filling
- 2 tablespoons olive oil
- ½ lb. beef sirloin, cut into ¼-inch pieces
- ½ lb. pork tenderloin, cut into ¼-inch pieces
- 1 medium onion, chopped
- 1 garlic clove, finely chopped
- 1 (14½-oz.) can diced tomatoes, drained
- 1 tart apple, chopped
- ¼ cup chopped green bell pepper
- ¼ cup golden raisins
- 2 teaspoons chili powder
- 1 teaspoon ground coriander
- ½ teaspoon ground cumin
- ½ teaspoon cinnamon
- ¼ teaspoon ground allspice
- ⅛ teaspoon anise seed

Tamale Dough
- 2¼ cups masa harina (dehydrated masa flour)
- ½ cup plus 1 tablespoon lard or vegetable shortening
- 1 teaspoon salt
- 1½ cups water
- 18 dried corn husks, soaked in warm water 1 hour, drained, dried

1. In large skillet, heat oil over medium-high heat until hot. Sauté beef, pork, onion and garlic over medium-high heat until meat is no longer pink in center. Stir in remaining filling ingredients; sauté 10 minutes or until apple and bell pepper are tender. Transfer mixture to bowl; cover and refrigerate. Filling can be prepared up to 2 days ahead.

2. In large bowl, mix masa harina, lard and salt until well blended. Stir in water; beat with wooden spoon until dough is stiff enough to spread. Spread each corn husk with about 2 tablespoons tamale dough, making rectangle about 4x3 inches. Spoon about 3 tablespoons meat filling down center of tamale dough. Fold ends of husk over, enclosing filling. Roll husk to form round tamale. Tie tamales in center with strips of soaked husk. Tamales can be frozen at this point.

3. Place tamales on rack in large pot or in steamer over lightly boiling water. Steam 30 to 35 minutes (adding more boiling water to pot as needed) or until tamales are firm to the touch but not hard, and dough comes away easily from husk. To serve, open husks; pass salsa to spoon over tamales.

6 servings (18 tamales)

SALSA VERDE

Tomatillos—husked green tomatoes grown in Mexico—have a tartness that is refreshing in salsas and salads. Their pale green color provides a visual counterpoint to red tomato salsas, as does their taste. To use, remove the papery husk and rinse off the sticky film that coats the fruit. This salsa is best served the day it's made, but it will keep for a day or so if refrigerated with plastic wrap pressed onto surface.

1   lb. fresh tomatillos, husks removed, rinsed
⅓   cup coarsely chopped white onion
3   jalapeño chiles, seeded, quartered
2   garlic cloves, peeled, halved
⅓   cup packed fresh cilantro leaves
¼   cup fresh lime juice
2   ripe avocados, peeled, cut into ¼-inch pieces
¼   teaspoon salt

1. Cut tomatillos in quarters. Place in food processor with remaining ingredients except avocados and salt. Process until pureed. Stir in avocado. Season with salt.

3 cups

PLAN-AHEAD TIPS

To throw a tamale party, plan ahead and have the picadillo filling made.

☀ Make the Salsa Verde, but wait to stir in the avocado until serving time.

☀ Prepare the Taos Supper Salad, and let it marinate in the refrigerator while the tamale-making is going on.

☀ The Frozen Margarita Mousses can be prepared days ahead, ready to pull out of the freezer anytime.

☀ Soak the corn husks, set up work stations.

☀ Put on some great music and your family and guests will be ready to work, laugh, talk and have fun!

Salsa Verde

Taos Supper Salad

TAOS SUPPER SALAD

Chayote, a pale green pear-shaped squash, is tender like zucchini when cooked. It's common in Mexican cooking, but is also known as mirilton and is often served stuffed in the southern part of the United States. Sprinkle hulled green pumpkin seeds or toasted pine nuts on top for a tasty garnish.

2 chayote squash (about 1¼ lb.), peeled,
     cut into ½-inch cubes
2 medium oranges
1 medium jicama (about 1 lb.), cut into ½-inch cubes
1 small red or yellow bell pepper, cut into thin strips
4 green onions, thinly sliced
¼ cup sherry or red wine vinegar
2 tablespoons olive oil
2 tablespoons chopped fresh cilantro

1. In large saucepan, bring about 1½ quarts water to a boil. Add chayote; simmer about 10 minutes or until tender. Rinse under cold water; drain well.

2. Meanwhile, peel skin from oranges with a sharp paring knife. Cut orange segments from between membranes; place segments in large serving bowl along with juices from oranges. Add jicama, bell pepper strips and green onions.

3. Stir chayote cubes into salad bowl. In small bowl, whisk together vinegar, olive oil and cilantro. Pour over salad; toss well.

6 servings

Frozen Margarita Mousses with Strawberry-Mango Sauce

Individually molded frozen mousses are great to prepare ahead—spoon the mousse into custard cups or even large coffee cups to freeze the chiffon-like mixture. Take care to completely dissolve the gelatin and thoroughly blend it into the mousse base. Refrigerated egg product, which is basically egg whites, is used for food safety purposes because the egg is not being cooked.

⅔ cup whipping cream
1 teaspoon vanilla
2 (¼-oz.) pkg. unflavored gelatin
⅔ cup cold water
1 cup fat-free, cholesterol-free egg product
1 cup sugar
⅔ cup frozen limeade concentrate, thawed
2 teaspoons finely shredded orange peel
1 teaspoon finely shredded lime peel
2 tablespoons Tequila or orange juice
1 to 2 drops of green food color, if desired
1 (10-oz.) pkg. frozen sliced strawberries
    in light syrup, thawed
¾ cup sliced mango in syrup
Sugar 'n Salt Tortilla Wafers (see below)

1. Lightly butter and lightly sugar inside of 6 (6-oz.) custard cups or molds. In chilled bowl, beat whipping cream and vanilla at medium speed until soft peaks forms; refrigerate.

2. In small saucepan, sprinkle gelatin over cold water. Cook and stir over low heat just until gelatin dissolves.

3. Remove gelatin from heat; transfer to large bowl. Stir in egg product, sugar, limeade concentrate, orange and lime peels, ½ tablespoon of the Tequila and green food coloring. Refrigerate 5 to 6 minutes, stirring occasionally, until mixture begins to thicken.

4. Beat gelatin mixture at medium to high speed 4 minutes. Immediately fold in whipped cream mixture. Spoon into custard cups. Freeze at least 2 hours or up to 3 days.

5. Before serving mousse, place strawberries with syrup, mangoes, remaining 1½ tablespoons Tequila

and 1 tablespoon lime juice in food processor. Process until smooth.

6. To serve, dip bottoms of custard cups briefly in warm water. Run thin metal spatula around edges to loosen; turn out each mousse onto individual dessert plate. Spoon strawberry-mango sauce around each mousse. Serve with Sugar 'n Salt Tortilla Wafers.

8 servings

Frozen Margarita Mousses with Strawberry-Mango Sauce, served with Sugar 'n Salt Tortilla Wafers

Sugar 'n Salt Tortilla Wafers

¼ cup coarse sugar
1 teaspoon kosher (coarse) salt
6 (7-inch) flour tortillas
2 tablespoons butter, melted

1. Heat oven to 375°F. Combine sugar and salt in small bowl. Brush tortillas with butter. Sprinkle with sugar-salt mixture. Cut each tortilla into 6 wedges or cut out with cookie cutters. Place wedges on ungreased baking sheet. Bake 7 to 9 minutes or until golden brown and crisp.

6 servings

Trim the Tree

PARTY

by Lisa Golden Schroeder

At the center of homestyle entertaining is the return to the comfort food we all crave. A tree-trimming party is so traditional that a homey menu just seems to fit the bill. And soup seems to be at the top of everyone's comfort list, so here's a buffet that includes two soup offerings: smoky bean soup that tastes long-simmered and is soul satisfying, yet a breeze to make; and a chilled gazpacho, made from winter citrus juices, that makes a surprising and refreshing counterpart.

Parmesan Sunflower Scones are quick to bake and delicious, but if time is precious, search out unique breads, rolls and crackers to serve with flavored butters. Bagged organic salad greens make great salads; add winter fruits (grapefruit or orange segments,

Trim the Tree

PARTY

MENU

SMOKED CHICKEN-BEAN SOUP

WINTER GAZPACHO

PARMESAN SUNFLOWER SCONES

BUTTERSCOTCH-CASHEW
BREAD PUDDING

Serves 6

chopped apple or pear) or flavorful root vegetables like thin strips of celery root or jicama or Jerusalem artichoke, to add texture and crunch. Sprinkle with toasted nuts or dried fruits, and toss with a flavorful bottled dressing, such as sweet red wine or balsamic vinaigrette or poppy seed dressing. An interesting selection of cheeses would go well with this menu too.

Finally, a warm, gooey bread pudding tops off the line-up. Toasted cashews in caramel make this the ultimate comfort dessert. Now bring on the popcorn and cranberry garlands!

SMOKED CHICKEN-BEAN SOUP

Look for smoked poultry in the deli, along with Asiago cheese, to garnish this easy bean soup. Any combination of beans could be used—some garbanzo beans will add more texture and bite. A dollop of basil pesto adds a hint of freshness.

1   tablespoon olive oil
1   medium red onion, chopped
3   ribs celery, halved lengthwise, sliced
         crosswise into ½-inch pieces
3   garlic cloves, minced
5   cups reduced-sodium chicken broth
1   (14½-oz.) can diced tomatoes
         with Italian style herbs, undrained
2   cups diced butternut squash or sweet potato
1   tablespoon sliced fresh sage
         or 1½ teaspoons dried sage leaves, crumbled
¼   teaspoon celery seed
¼   teaspoon salt
¼   teaspoon freshly ground pepper
3   (15-oz.) cans cooked white beans
         rinsed, drained (about 6 cups)
12   oz. (¾-lb.) smoked chicken or turkey,
         cut into ½-inch pieces
½   cup prepared basil pesto
         Garlic croutons or shredded Asiago cheese,
            if desired

1. In a large pot or Dutch oven, heat oil over medium-high heat until hot; sauté onion, celery and garlic about 4 minutes or until vegetables are tender.

2. Pour broth into pot. Stir in tomatoes with juice, squash, sage, celery seed, salt and pepper. Bring mixture to a boil. Reduce heat to low. Partially cover pot; simmer 25 minutes or until squash is tender.

3. Stir beans and chicken into soup. Cook an additional 15 minutes. Serve hot, with a dollop of pesto swirled into each bowl. Top with one spoonful of croutons or cheese.

6 servings

WINTER GAZPACHO

Soup

5   ripe plum tomatoes, cut into quarters
2   green, red, or yellow bell peppers, cut into quarters
1   cucumber, cut into 1-inch pieces
4   green onions, cut into 1-inch pieces
2   garlic cloves, halved
2   cups tomato juice
1   cup fresh orange juice
¼   cup packed fresh cilantro leaves
3   tablespoons fresh lime juice
2   tablespoons extra-virgin olive oil
1½   teaspoons grated orange peel
½   teaspoon grated lime peel
¼   teaspoon salt
         Hot pepper sauce to taste

Condiment Suggestions

1   cup sour cream with 2 teaspoons lime juice stirred
         in (offer in a squeeze bottle)
     Toasted slivered almonds
     Cooked bay shrimp
     Coarsely chopped green or ripe olives
     Diced avocado
     Thin strips of toasted corn tortilla
         (toast in 400°F oven)

1. Place tomatoes, peppers, cucumber, onions and garlic in food processor or blender (process in batches in blender); coarsely chop. Transfer one-half of vegetable mixture to large bowl.

2. Add tomato juice, orange juice, cilantro, lime juice, olive oil and citrus peels to food processor. Process mixture until nearly smooth. Combine vegetable and juice mixtures.

3. Mix soup well; season with salt and hot pepper sauce. Serve chilled with selection of condiments.

6 to 8 servings

SOUP SERVING IDEAS

Arrange the various condiments for each soup around the main soup bowls or tureens. Have stacks of bowls, mugs or even margarita glasses to ladle the soups into, along with soup spoons and large linen napkins to protect laps if your guests are perching on couches or chairs. Trays on which to set bowls, bread, and salad will make serving and eating easier too.

Winter Gazpacho and Condiments

Large Margarita glasses filled with this well-chilled Winter Gazpacho will chase away any winter blues. This tangy version is made with winter citrus juices. Make the soup ahead so the flavors will develop. Offer a selection of any of the suggested condiments to spoon into each serving.

Trim the Tree Party

Parmesan Sunflower Scones and Smoked Chicken Bean Soup

PARMESAN SUNFLOWER SCONES

Scones, a traditional Scottish quick bread, have evolved in the past several years. Sweet, buttery scones are always served at tea time in Great Britain. Here, a savory version features pungent Parmesan cheese and rich sunflower seeds. Golden crisp on the outside, and biscuit-like inside, these are best eaten freshly made.

2	cups all-purpose flour
1	tablespoon baking powder
¼	cup plus 1 teaspoon grated freshly grated Parmesan cheese
½	cup cold butter, cut up
2	tablespoons unsalted sunflower seeds
	About ¾ cup buttermilk

1. Heat oven to 400°F. Spray large baking sheet with nonstick cooking spray. In medium bowl, combine flour, baking powder and ¼ cup of the cheese. With pastry blender or two knives, work butter into flour mixture until mixture forms pea-sized crumbs. Stir in sunflower seeds.

2. Add ½ cup buttermilk; stir in just enough to evenly moisten dough. If dough is crumbly, sprinkle a little more buttermilk over mixture and stir. Gather dough into ball; knead in bowl 10 to 12 times or until almost smooth.

3. Place dough on baking sheet. Flatten into a round ½-inch thick. With floured knife, cut round into eighths, leaving wedges in place. Brush dough with 2 teaspoons buttermilk; sprinkle with remaining 1 teaspoon Parmesan cheese.

4. Bake 20 to 25 minutes or until golden brown. Transfer to a wire rack. Break round into wedges. Serve warm or cool.

8 scones

BUTTERSCOTCH-CASHEW BREAD PUDDING

To truly gild the lily on this homey, gooey dessert, scoop some vanilla bean ice cream onto each serving of pudding before drizzling on the Butterscotch-Cashew Sauce. The bit of salt on the cashews intensifies the sauce's caramel flavor.

Bread Pudding

¼	cup butter
4	cups (about 8 oz.) fresh French bread cubes (¾-inch pieces)
2	cups milk
½	cup packed brown sugar
3	eggs, slightly beaten
1	teaspoon rum extract

Butterscotch-Cashew Sauce

¼	cup butter
½	cup coarsely chopped salted cashews
½	cup light corn syrup
½	cup packed brown sugar
2	tablespoons water
¼	cup whipping cream

1. Heat oven to 350°F. Place butter in 2-quart casserole; melt butter in oven. Remove from oven; add bread cubes and toss to coat.

2. In medium bowl, combine milk, brown sugar, eggs and rum extract; blend well. Pour over bread cubes. Bake 55 to 60 minutes or until center is set. Serve pudding with warm Butterscotch-Cashew Sauce.

3. To prepare sauce, in medium skillet, melt butter over medium-low heat. Add cashews; sauté 3 minutes. Carefully stir in corn syrup, brown sugar and water. Cook and stir until sugar is dissolved. Stir in cream. Bring to a boil; reduce heat to low. Boil gently, uncovered, 5 minutes. Serve warm over bread pudding.

6 servings

Butterscotch-Cashew Bread Pudding and Smoked Chicken-Bean Soup (recipe on page 94)

Trim the Tree Party

Formal

CHRISTMAS DINNER

by Carole Brown

We've created this special menu for a Christmas dinner party —sophisticated and festive—but based on cozy and inviting home cooking. It will work well for six to eight people.

Nothing says "Happy Holidays" like a glass of bubbly. Welcome your guests with a glass of Champagne —our Cranberry Sparklers, blushing with a torch of cranberry. And what could be merrier than a holiday platter bearing a succulent Standing Rib Roast of Beef? To accompany the beef, we propose a toasty Gratin of Potato and Celery Root, and a colorful stack of Carrots, Parsnips and Leeks Julienne.

Formal
CHRISTMAS DINNER

MENU

CRANBERRY SPARKLERS

SALMON SPREAD

CUCUMBER RIBBONS IN MUSTARD VINAIGRETTE

STANDING RIB ROAST

GRATIN OF POTATO AND CELERY ROOT

CARROTS, PARSNIPS AND LEEKS JULIENNE

BUCHE DE NOEL, CHRISTMAS YULE LOG CAKE

Serves 8

To make your entertaining schedule easier, you can prepare many of these dishes in advance, such as the Salmon Spread and Cucumber Ribbons for the first course.

For a special holiday dessert, nobody can resist the French cake Bûche de Noël, or Christmas Yule Log Cake. It's a sponge cake that is rolled and spread with Chocolate Mocha Icing to resemble a log on the forest floor, with each slice revealing a tempting swirl of cake and icing.

CRANBERRY SPARKLERS

Choose a brut Champagne or any other dry sparkling wine for this aperitif. Don't overfill the glasses—about two thirds full is just right for sparkling wine.

8   tablespoons thawed cranberry juice concentrate
3   tablespoons orange liqueur
I   bottle chilled dry sparkling wine

I. Mix together cranberry juice concentrate and orange liqueur, divide it equally among 8 Champagne flutes. Fill glasses with sparkling wine and serve.

6 to 8 aperitifs

Cranberry Sparkler

SALMON SPREAD

This elegant salmon spread is ideal for entertaining because it actually should be made a day or two in advance. It uses fresh poached salmon with some smoked salmon as a flavor accent. The smoother texture of cold-smoked salmon, or lox, is slightly better in this recipe, but the more flaky, hot-smoked salmon could also be used. Work the spread together by hand with a fork or pulse it in a food processor, but be careful not to overwork it, as this would make it too smooth and pasty.

Salmon

I   cup water
I   cup white wine
½   teaspoon salt
8   oz. trimmed skinless fillet of salmon

Spread

½   cup (4 oz.) cream cheese
3   tablespoons lemon juice
¼   teaspoon salt
⅛   teaspoon freshly ground pepper
½   cup smoked salmon or lox, diced
3   tablespoons chopped fresh dill
       or 2 teaspoons dried dill weed
12 slices pumpernickel bread
       Dill sprigs

I. In medium saucepan, combine water, wine and salt; bring to a simmer. Immerse salmon fillet in simmering liquid; turn off heat. Let stand 5 to 8 minutes, or until salmon just begins to flake. Remove from liquid. Place on clean kitchen towel to drain and cool. Break salmon into 1½ cups coarse flakes; refrigerate.

2. In food processor, combine cream cheese, lemon juice, salt and pepper; process briefly to blend. Add flaked salmon; pulse 6 to 8 times. Add diced smoked salmon; pulse several times until smoked salmon is roughly incorporated into cream cheese mixture. Remove to bowl; stir in chopped dill. Refrigerate salmon spread for several hours or overnight before serving.

3. Heat broiler. Trim crusts off bread; cut each slice into 2 or 4 triangular pieces. Arrange pieces on baking sheet; toast briefly under broiler. Set aside to accompany salmon spread.

4. To serve, divide salmon spread evenly among serving plates (an oval or round ice-cream scoop will help you make an attractive presentation) or pack spread into individual ramekins. Garnish with the dill sprigs, Cucumber Ribbons and pumpernickel toast points.

CUCUMBER RIBBONS IN MUSTARD VINAIGRETTE

Cucumbers are a classical flavor match with salmon. The long ribbons make an unusual presentation for a special occasion, but you can size them into thin rounds if you prefer. Salting the cucumbers will keep them crisp.

2   large cucumbers, ends trimmed, peeled
½   teaspoon kosher (coarse) salt
2   tablespoons white wine vinegar
⅛   teaspoon salt
⅛   teaspoon freshly ground pepper
2   teaspoons Dijon mustard
6   tablespoons extra-virgin olive oil
3   tablespoons chopped parsley

I. Cut cucumber lengthwise into long thin slices with vegetable peeler, sharp cheese slicer or mandolin, cutting as many ribbons as you can until you reach inner core of seeds, about 10 to 15 ribbons. Put ribbons into colander and sprinkle lightly with salt; let stand 30 to 60 minutes. Meanwhile, prepare vinaigrette.

2. In small bowl, combine vinegar, salt, pepper and mustard; mix well to dissolve salt. Whisk in olive oil.

3. Rinse cucumber ribbons briefly; drain and wrap in clean kitchen towel to dry. Toss with vinaigrette. Serve immediately or refrigerate several hours.

About 8 servings

Cucumber Ribbons in Mustard Vinaigrette

Standing Rib Roast

STANDING RIB ROAST

For generous dinner servings plus some leftovers, choose a 3-bone roast for 6 people and a 4-bone roast for 8 people, between 5½ and 7 pounds. If you prefer, serve a boneless rolled rib roast; plan on 6 to 8 ounces per serving, or 4 to 5 pounds. Talk to your butcher well in advance and ask for a roast from the loin end of the ribs (not the shoulder end); this will give you the best and most tender rib eye. To make the roast easy to carve, be sure the butcher removes the backbone.

Trim away all but a thin layer of fat from the top of the roast (a rolled roast will probably be tied and ready for the oven). Remove the meat from the refrigerator 1 to 2 hours before baking. Baking time will be 1½ to 2 hours, plus 30 minutes of resting time before carving. Choose a low-sided metal roasting pan that is generous in size for your roast and can be used on a range-top burner to make gravy (or pan juice). Make sure the roasting pan fits in the oven with the pan you will use for the Gratin of Potato and Celery Root; they will share the oven for about 30 minutes.

STANDING RIB ROAST

For many people, the most intimidating aspect of a large roast is knowing when it is done. We recommend using an instant-read thermometer. The USDA recommends cooking all beef to a temperature of at least 160°F. At this temperature, the meat will be medium with a slightly pink center. Remember that the end cuts of the roast will be slightly more done than the center, and the meat will continue to cook a bit more during its 30-minute rest period.

3 or 4-bone standing rib roast
or 4-to 5-lb. boneless rolled rib roast
1 tablespoon salt
1 tablespoon freshly ground pepper
2 tablespoons all-purpose flour
2 cups meat or vegetable broth

1. Heat oven to 450°F. Rub roast all over with salt and pepper. Stand roast on its bones in low-sided roasting pan; put pan in oven. After 15 minutes, reduce oven temperature to 350°F. Bake 45 to 60 minutes; check internal temperature of roast with an instant-read thermometer. Continue checking meat at 10-minute intervals until it reaches your desired temperature. Remove from oven; transfer to platter. Cover loosely with aluminum foil; set aside to rest 30 minutes.

2. To prepare pan juice (au jus) to serve on meat, pour off all fat from roasting pan. Place pan over burner on top of range; pour in broth. Simmer 3 to 5 minutes as you scrape up browned bits from bottom of pan. Taste and season with salt and pepper if necessary; strain jus into serving boat.

3. OR...To prepare gravy, pour off all but 2 tablespoons fat from roasting pan. Place pan over burner on top of range and heat over medium heat. Add flour; whisk into fat. Simmer 2 to 3 minutes as you whisk and scrape up browned bits from bottom of pan. Add broth; simmer 5 to 10 minutes. Season with salt and pepper. If desired, strain gravy into serving boat.

4. To carve, cut meat away from bones. Stand meat horizontally and cut slices downward. You may prefer to lay meat on its side and slice sideways, cutting thick or thin slices according to your guests' preferences.

About 8 servings

GRATIN OF POTATO AND CELERY ROOT

Individually, potatoes and celery root are delicious winter vegetables, but in this recipe they are even better together! We have replaced one-half of the traditional cream with broth; this lets the flavors of the potatoes and celery root shine through. You can peel the potatoes and celery root in advance, but hold them submerged in water to prevent them from discoloring until you are ready to slice them and assemble the gratin.

The gratin should go into the oven about 30 minutes before the rib roast is due to come out. Then it can finish baking while the roast is resting. Like a roast, a vegetable gratin is easier to slice and serve after it has rested a few minutes.

1 to 2 tablespoons butter, softened
1 to 2 garlic cloves, minced
3 potatoes (about 2 lb.), peeled
3 large (1 lb. each) celery root (celeriac), peeled
1 teaspoon salt
1 teaspoon freshly ground white pepper
2 cups vegetable or chicken broth
2 cups whipping cream

1. Heat oven to 350°F. Spread butter in 13x9-inch pan. Smear garlic on bottom and sides of pan.

2. Cut both potatoes and celery root into thin, similar-sized slices. Spread vegetables in alternating layers in dish, sprinkling each layer with salt and pepper. Mix broth and cream; pour liquid into dish until it is level with top of vegetables.

3. Bake about 60 minutes until vegetables are well cooked and top is browned. Baste top with cooking liquid 2 to 3 times during the first 30 minutes. Remove gratin from oven; cover loosely with aluminum foil. Allow to rest 10 to 15 minutes before serving.

About 8 servings

Bûche de Noël, Christmas Youe Log Cake

CARROTS, PARSNIPS AND LEEKS JULIENNE

Delicate julienne slices of vegetables cook quickly, and you can give your dinner plate a dressed-up party look by serving them mounded high in a stack. Cut them by hand or with a mandolin slicer. If you prefer, you can slice the vegetables into thin rounds. For easier entertaining, use an old chef's trick here—braise the vegetables in advance until they are almost done; cool and refrigerate. Then sauté vegetables at the last minute. The carrots take slightly longer to cook than the parsnips and leeks, so give them a head start by cooking them alone for a couple of minutes.

4 carrots, peeled
3 parsnips, peeled
3 leeks
¾ cup water
¼ teaspoon salt
2 tablespoons butter
2 tablespoons dry vermouth or white wine
¾ teaspoon ground ginger
½ teaspoon salt
½ teaspoon freshly ground pepper
2 to 3 tablespoons chopped fresh parsley

1. Cut carrots and parsnips into 1½-inch lengths, then cut each piece into thin slices. Stack 2 or 3 slices at a time and cut stack into thin strips.

2. To prepare leeks, trim away roots, dark green upper leaves and any dirty or dry outside layers. Slice each leek in half lengthwise, stopping about 1-inch above root end; this will hold leek together, making it easier to handle. Rinse each leek well under running water to remove any grit from between layers. Shake excess water from leeks; wrap briefly in clean kitchen towel to dry. Finish cutting each leek in half lengthwise; cut each half into 1½-inch lengths. Slice each of these pieces

3. In covered skillet, bring water and ¼ teaspoon salt to a simmer over medium heat. Add carrots; cover and cook 2 minutes. Add leeks and parsnips, using tongs or cooking spoon to toss and mix with carrots. Cover and cook an additional 2 minutes or until almost cooked, turning vegetables once. Vegetables should no longer be crunchy, but should retain some texture. Drain vegetables; spread out on baking sheet to facilitate quick cooling. The recipe may be prepared ahead to this point; refrigerate cooled vegetables until you are ready to sauté and serve.

4. In large skillet, heat butter over medium heat until melted; add vermouth, ginger, salt and pepper. Simmer until most of vermouth has evaporated. Add vegetables and toss over medium heat until hot. Stir in parsley before serving.

About 8 servings

Buche De Noel, Christmas Yule Log Cake

You can chill Bûche de Noël for several hours before serving, but it is best served cool or at room temperature. To bring it to room temperature, and a softer texture, take the cake out of the refrigerator just before dinner to use as a centerpiece.

Cake
¾ cup all-purpose flour
2 tablespoons sugar
⅛ teaspoon salt
4 eggs
2 egg yolks
¾ cup sugar
1½ teaspoons vanilla

Chocolate Mocha Icing
2 cups whipping cream
6 tablespoons light corn syrup
3 tablespoons instant espresso or coffee powder
8 oz. semisweet chocolate, cut into ¼-inch pieces

Garnish
2 tablespoons ground walnuts or unsalted pistachios
Powdered sugar
Unsweetened cocoa

1. Heat oven to 350°F. Spray 15x10-inch jellyroll pan with nonstick cooking spray. Line pan with parchment paper, allowing 2 to 3 inches of excess paper on each end of pan; you will use extra paper to lift cake out of pan after baking. Spray paper and lightly flour.

2. In small bowl stir together flour, 2 tablespoons sugar and salt; set aside.

3. In large bowl, beat together whole eggs, egg yolks, ¾ cup sugar and vanilla until mixture has tripled in volume, is light in color and holds a thick ribbon for several seconds.

4. Gradually sift and fold one-third of the flour mixture into batter; fold until thoroughly combined. Do not overmix. Repeat with remaining two thirds flour mixture.

5. Pour mixture into pan gently spreading evenly. Bake 12 to 14 minutes or until cake springs back when touched and top is light golden brown. Cool 5 minutes. Run small knife around edge of pan to loosen cake. Using ends of parchment paper, lift cake onto wire rack. Cool completely.

6. To prepare icing, in medium saucepan, combine cream, corn syrup and espresso powder; bring just to a boil. Stir well to dissolve espresso. In large bowl, pour cream mixture over chocolate. Swirl gently to melt chocolate. Whisk until chocolate is blended. Strain mixture. Cool, stirring occasionally. Cover and refrigerate several hours or overnight.

7. Just before frosting cake, beat icing at medium speed until lighter in color and spreadable, being careful not to overwhip, causing cream to separate.

8. Move cake to flat surface; spread with one-half of Chocolate Mocha Icing, about 1¼ cups. Starting at long edge, roll cake into log, gently releasing parchment paper as you go. Transfer cake to serving platter. Trim ends of cake by making diagonal slices at each end. Choose better-looking slice; dab some icing on its underside. Position it slightly off-center on top of log to resemble sawed-off branch.

9. Spread remaining icing on outside and ends of log. Spread icing up to cover seam and sides of "branch." Create the look of bark by dragging fork through icing.

10. Sprinkle ground nuts around base of cake and on platter. Refrigerate cake several hours before serving. Finish decorating by lightly sifting powdered sugar on platter and edges of cake. Garnish with cranberry and rosemary sprigs. Top powdered sugar with light dusting of cocoa. Cut cake into diagonal slices before serving. Store in refrigerator.

8-10 servings

CHRISTMAS

Tea Party

by Mary Evans

CHRISTMAS

Tea Party

MENU

TRIPLE TOMATO
OPEN-FACED SANDWICHES

EGG SALAD SANDWICHES

CURRANT SCONES

CUCUMBER TREE SANDWICHES

TIRAMISU MINI CREAM PUFFS

CRANBERRY-LEMON
CURD TARTLETS

Serves 8

The holidays don't always have to be about big, formal sit-down meals. How about a smaller, lighter, more intimate gathering like this Christmas Tea Party? The sandwiches are delightful and festive, the sweets just right for an afternoon gathering.

The sandwiches suggested here can be supplemented with others. Try Stilton or blue cheese on buttered raisin bread or smoke salmon and cream cheese sandwiches. Feel free to use your own favorite sandwich fixings, working off the basic ideas here. If you need to save some time, purchase miniature pastries from your favorite bakery instead of baking your own.

TRIPLE TOMATO OPEN-FACED SANDWICHES

Using holiday cookie cutters makes these finger sandwiches more festive. If you're not a fan of goat cheese, use cream cheese instead. If your market sells olive bread, try that instead of white.

8	oz. mild goat cheese
¼	cup finely chopped sun-dried tomatoes
1	tablespoon tomato paste
½	teaspoon dried Italian seasoning
4	slices firm white sandwich bread
16	thin slices plum tomatoes
1	teaspoon finely chopped parsley

1. In medium bowl, blend together goat cheese, sun-dried tomatoes, tomato paste and Italian seasoning. Thin with a few drops milk if necessary to bring to spreading consistency. Spread mixture over bread slices. Cut each slice with 1½-inch round cutter or small ornament-shaped cookie cutter into four circles or shapes.

2. Top with tomato slice; garnish with finely chopped parsley to form ornament top.

8 servings

EGG SALAD SANDWICHES

The butter seals the bread and keeps it from getting soggy when sandwiches are made in advance. If made ahead, store covered with a barely damp towel topped with plastic wrap.

3	hard boiled eggs, finely chopped
3	tablespoons mayonnaise
1	tablespoon capers, chopped
2	teaspoons finely chopped green onion
¾	teaspoon Dijon mustard
⅛	teaspoon salt
⅛	teaspoon freshly ground pepper
8	thin slices firm white sandwich bread
⅓	cup butter, softened
⅔	cup finely chopped parsley

1. In medium bowl, combine eggs, mayonnaise, capers, green onion, mustard, salt and pepper; mix until well blended.

2. Spread 1 teaspoon butter on each slice of bread. Top each of 4 bread slices, butter side up, with ¼ of the egg salad mixture. Cover with remaining 4 bread slices, butter side down.

3. Trim crusts from bread; cut each sandwich in quarters. Spread remaining butter along edges of each quarter. Dip buttered edges in parsley.

8 servings

CURRANT SCONES

These are best served fresh from the oven, but can be made earlier in the day and briefly reheated.

2¼   cups all-purpose flour
½   cup powdered sugar
1 ½   teaspoons baking powder
½   teaspoon baking soda
½   teaspoon salt
¼   cup unsalted butter, chilled, cut in ½-inch pieces
¼   cup sour cream
¼   cup plus 1 teaspoon milk
1   egg
¼   cup currants
1   tablespoon sugar

1. Heat oven to 425°F. Line baking sheet with parchment paper.

2. In food processor, combine flour, powdered sugar, baking powder, baking soda and salt; pulse several times. Add butter and process about 15 seconds or until pieces of butter are no longer visible. In small bowl, beat together sour cream, ¼ cup milk and egg; add to food processor and process about 15 seconds to form coarse dough.

3. Turn dough out onto lightly floured surface. Sprinkle with currants and gently knead 6 to 8 times to combine. Roll dough out to about ½-inch thickness. Cut dough into circles using a 2-inch cutter; place on baking sheet. Brush dough with 1 teaspoon milk; sprinkle with sugar. Bake 10 to 12 minutes or until lightly browned. Serve warm with clotted cream or butter and jam.

16 scones

CUCUMBER TREE SANDWICHES

Burpless or English cucumbers are used here because they have no seeds and make an attractive presentation.

4   oz. cream cheese, softened
1   tablespoon finely chopped fresh dill weed
1   tablespoon finely chopped parsley
2   teaspoons finely chopped chives
¼   teaspoon celery salt
4   slices firm white sandwich bread
1   seedless cucumber
24   dill sprigs for garnish

1. Mix cream cheese, dill, parsley, chives and celery salt together in medium bowl. Thin with a few drops lemon juice or milk if necessary to bring to spreading consistency. Spread over bread slices.

2. Cut each bread slice into 6 trees using small (about 1 x 1½-inch) tree cookie cutter.

3. Cut cucumber into chunks that match length of the cookie cutter. Cut thin lengthwise strips from each chunk and cut each strip with tree cookie cutter. Place cucumber tree on top of each sandwich cutout. Or, trim crusts from bread; top with thinly cut slices cucumber. Cut in half crosswise and cut each half into 3 elongated triangles. Garnish with dill sprigs if desired.

8 servings

Currant Scones

TIRAMISU MINI CREAM PUFFS

Tiramisu is a classic Italian dessert. We've borrowed some of the traditional flavors of mascarpone, coffee and rum to make a wonderful cream puff filling. The unfilled cream puffs can be made ahead and frozen. Bake at 350°F about 5 minutes to re-crisp. Fill the puffs no more than two hours in advance.

Cream Puffs

½ cup water
¼ cup butter
⅛ teaspoon salt
½ cup all-purpose flour
2 eggs

Tiramisu Filling

8 oz. Mascarpone cheese
¼ cup sugar
½ cup heavy whipping cream
2 teaspoons instant espresso powder
2 tablespoons dark rum
1½ teaspoons unsweetened cocoa

1. Heat oven to 400°F. Line baking sheet with parchment paper.

2. In small saucepan, heat water, butter and salt over medium high heat until mixture comes to a full boil, making sure butter is fully melted. Remove from heat; stir in flour. Return to medium heat and continue to cook, stirring constantly, until mixture comes together in a ball and leaves a thin film on bottom of pan. Remove from heat and let cool 5 minutes. Beat in eggs one at a time, stirring after each addition until fully incorporated. Drop in 1½-inch mounds on baking sheet. Bake 20 minutes or until puffed and browned.

3. Remove from oven and prick sides of each puff with tip of knife. Return to oven 5 minutes to dry slightly. Remove; cool on wire rack.

4. In medium bowl, beat together mascarpone and sugar at medium speed about 1 minute or until blended. Dissolve espresso in whipping cream; add to mascarpone. Beat about 2 minutes or until mixture is thick and holds its shape. Stir in rum.

5. Cut cream puffs in half; fill with mascarpone mixture. Place cocoa in very fine strainer and dust tops of puffs lightly. Refrigerate leftovers.

16 cream puffs

TEA VARIETIES

❧ Black teas are fermented, or oxidized, and include such well-known varieties as Ceylon, Darjeeling, English breakfast and orange pekoe. Earl Grey is a black tea that contains oil of bergamot to give it a distinctive flavor. Another black tea with a pronounced smoky flavor is Lapsang Souchong.

❧ Oolong teas are sometimes referred to as red teas. They are not as oxidized and have little caffeine.

❧ Green teas are also low in caffeine and are steamed to prevent fermentation. Jasmine and gunpowder tea are both green teas.

❧ Herbal teas, sometimes called infusions or tisanes, contain no tea at all, but are flavorful and said to have a variety of beneficial properties depending on the variety. They are also caffeine-free.

Cranberry-Lemon Curd Tartlets

CRANBERRY-LEMON CURD TARTLETS

If miniature tartlet pans are unavailable, use mini-muffin pans instead.

Crust
- ¾ cup all-purpose flour
- ¼ teaspoon salt
- ⅓ cup cold butter, chilled, cut up
- 6 to 8 teaspoons ice water

Filling
- ½ cup cranberries
- ⅓ cup water
- ¼ cup freshly squeezed lemon juice
- 4 to 5 drops red food color
- ¼ cup butter
- 2 eggs
- ⅔ cup sugar
- 1 teaspoon cornstarch
- ¼ cup sweetened whipped cream
- 16 dried cranberries

1. In medium bowl, combine flour and salt. Work in butter until mixture crumbles. Toss with ice water, using just enough to bring mixture together in a ball. Wrap in plastic wrap; flatten to form disk. Refrigerate 1 hour.

2. Heat oven to 400°F. Roll out dough ¼-inch thick on lightly floured surface. Cut dough using 2½-inch round cutter; press into 16 (2-inch) round tartlet pans. Line each with aluminum foil and weight with dried beans or pie weights.

3. Bake 12 minutes; remove foil and weights. Return to oven; bake an additional 8 to 10 minutes or until lightly browned and crisp. Let cool completely; remove from pans.

4. In small saucepan, bring cranberries and ⅓ cup water to a boil over medium heat; continue to boil 4 minutes. Cranberries will soften and most of water will evaporate. Strain into small bowl; press lightly against cranberries to extract juices. Measure 1 tablespoon liquid into medium saucepan; add lemon juice and food color. Stir to combine. Add butter; bring to a boil over medium heat, melting butter completely.

5. In medium bowl, whisk eggs in medium bowl with sugar and cornstarch. Slowly whisk in cranberry-lemon mixture. Return to saucepan; cook over low heat 5 to 8 minutes, stirring constantly, until mixture thickens. Do not boil. Immediately pour into medium bowl; cover and refrigerate until cold and thickened. To serve, spoon mixture into cooled tartlet shells. Top with dollop of whipped cream and dried cranberry. Refrigerate leftovers.

8 servings

CHRISTMAS
Brunch
by Ethel G. Hofman

Holiday celebrations seem to begin earlier each year. From the beginning of December, it's a mad whirl of office parties, department dinners, catered cocktail events and get-togethers of all kinds. But come Christmas day, it's time to relax a little and celebrate with family. The tree is sparkling with tinsel and bright ornaments, carefully wrapped gifts are torn or gently opened (depending on who is doing the opening), and there's excitement and anticipation in the air.

Gather friends and family around and serve up a glorious brunch buffet. No matter when you serve it—Christmas day or any other time during the holidays—it's the perfect way to say "Merry Christmas." Let them come downstairs in pajamas or arrive in jeans. And with the fun and informal menu following, even the host or hostess need not get up early.

Of course, like every other event held in the home, everybody is bound to congregate in the kitchen, where fragrant coffee is perking and water is on the boil for tea. Accept all offers to help. Guests love to chop, stir and garnish, leaving the cook to direct the delicious proceedings from kitchen to table—and accept rave reviews.

CHRISTMAS

Brunch

MENU

TOASTED CROISSANTS STUFFED
WITH SCRAMBLED EGGS AND OYSTERS

CARAMEL BAKED FRENCH TOAST

LEMON CLOUD TARTLETS

CRYSTAL COFFEE CAKE

CHOCOLATE TRUFFLE TRIFLE

Serves 8

MENU SUGGESTIONS

Hot Buttered Rum or Mulled Wine

Blueberry Sauce (for French Toast)

Smoked Salmon, Sliced Onion,
Tomatoes and Capers

Shrimp Bowl with Cocktail Sauce

Thinly Sliced Whole Wheat Bread,
Warm Rolls, Bagels and Sweet Butter

Asparagus Spears and Carrot Sticks
in a Basket, Herb Dip

Coffee, Tea and Hot Chocolate

Toasted Croissants Stuffed with Scrambled Eggs and Oysters

TOASTED CROISSANTS STUFFED WITH
SCRAMBLED EGGS AND OYSTERS

A breakfast sandwich you'll be pleased to serve…and your guests will love to eat.

  6 tablespoons butter
12 eggs
  1 cup milk
  2 tablespoons all-purpose flour
  1 teaspoon salt
  ½ teaspoon curry powder
  2 (3½-oz.) cans tiny smoked oysters, drained
  2 tablespoons finely chopped parsley
  8 croissants, split, toasted

1. In large skillet, melt butter over medium-low heat. In large bowl, whisk eggs, milk, flour, salt and curry powder. Pour into skillet; stir from outside edge to center, allowing uncooked eggs to flow to outer edge of skillet.

2. When eggs are almost set, fold in oysters and parsley. Continue stirring until mixture is creamy. Divide evenly among croissants, pressing down tops lightly.

8 servings

CARAMEL BAKED FRENCH TOAST

They'll never guess that this could be prepared with leftover bread. Crisp-crusted, sweet and scented with ginger and orange, this ideal brunch dish never fails to get rave reviews. Serve with a bowl of fruit salad or fresh orange sections.

    6   tablespoons unsalted butter,
          chilled, cut into 6 pieces
    ¾   cup packed brown sugar
    2   teaspoons orange infused oil
    1½ tablespoons grated fresh ginger
    8   (1-inch-thick) slices egg bread
    4   eggs
    2   cups milk
    1   teaspoon vanilla
    2   tablespoons cinnamon sugar

1. Place butter in microwave-safe 9-inch square glass baking dish. Microwave on medium 1 minute or until butter is melted. Stir in brown sugar and orange oil. Sprinkle with grated ginger.

2. Arrange bread slices on top in single layer. In medium bowl, whisk together eggs, milk and vanilla. Pour over bread, pressing down on bread to soak up egg mixture. Sprinkle with cinnamon sugar. Cover with plastic wrap and refrigerate overnight.

3. Heat oven to 375°F. Bake 10 minutes. Reduce heat to 350°F and bake 35 to 45 minutes or until puffed, golden brown and firm in center. Serve immediately.

8 servings

LEMON CLOUD TARTLETS

The lemon curd may be prepared days ahead. Meringues are added just before filling the shells. Mini phyllo dough shells may be found in the supermarket freezer section with baked goods.

    3   eggs
    ⅔   cup sugar
          Juice and grated peel of 1½ lemons
    4   tablespoons butter, melted
    ¾   cup crumbled meringue cookies
    1   (2-oz.) pkg. mini phyllo dough shells
          Strawberries, thinly sliced
          Mint leaves

PLAN-AHEAD TIPS

Planning ahead makes this spectacular Christmas brunch so easy. Don't hesitate to purchase convenient prepared items. In fact, everything following is available in your supermarket. It's one stop shopping! And most items (other than perishables such as whipping cream, parsley and mint) may be purchased a week or so in advance, thus avoiding a last-minute frenzy.

Most of the dishes in this menu are created to cook or assemble ahead.

- Prepare the Caramel Baked French Toast up to 24 hours ahead. Then all that remains is to transfer it from refrigerator to heated oven about 1 hour before serving.

- Crystal Coffee Cake (page 122), baked without the glaze and mixed fruits, may be wrapped in aluminum foil and refrigerated. Before serving, warm through in a heated 300°F oven 10 to 15 minutes, then decorate according to recipe directions.

- The same applies to the Chocolate Truffle Trifle (page 122) and Lemon Cloud Tartlets (page 121). Assemble the trifle the night before but decorate and garnish on Christmas morning. Lemon curd keeps well up to one week in the refrigerator. An hour or so before serving, just fold in the meringue, spoon into the tartlets and garnish.

1. To prepare lemon curd in blender, combine eggs, sugar, lemon juice and rind; blend 10 seconds. With motor running, slowly pour in melted butter.

2. Transfer to small, heavy-bottomed pan. Cook about 5 minutes over medium-high heat, whisking constantly, until mixture is thick enough to coat back of spoon. Pour into bowl; refrigerate. Fold in cookies.

3. Spoon into phyllo dough shells; garnish with strawberry slice and mint leaf. Store in refrigerator up to 6 hours before serving. Refrigerate leftovers.

15 tartlets

Crystal Coffee Cake

CRYSTAL COFFEE CAKE

For a crowd, double the ingredients and bake in two loaf pans. Use leftover beaten egg to add to breakfast items such as omelettes, scrambled eggs or pancakes.

1   (12-oz.) tube refrigerated flaky biscuits
⅓   cup raspberry cake and pastry filling
1   (3-oz.) bar white chocolate, cut into 10 pieces
2   tablespoons beaten egg
1   to 1½ teaspoons milk
2   tablespoons powered sugar
2   tablespoons glazed mixed fruits

1. Heat oven to 400°F. Spray 9x5-inch loaf pan with nonstick cooking spray. Separate biscuits, then separate each biscuit into two layers. In center of one layer, place rounded teaspoon of raspberry filling and a piece of white chocolate. Cover with remaining layer, pressing edges to seal; repeat with remaining biscuits, filling and white chocolate.

2. Arrange in loaf pan, pressing together to make a single layer. Brush with beaten egg. Bake 15 minutes or until deep golden brown. Cool in pan 2 minutes. Turn out onto wire rack.

3. To prepare glaze, in small bowl, stir milk into powdered sugar until thin enough to drizzle. Drizzle over warm coffee cake. Sprinkle with glazed fruits. Cool slightly before slicing with serrated knife.

8 servings

CHOCOLATE TRUFFLE TRIFLE

Chocolate truffle bars such as Lindt may be found in the supermarket candy aisles. Double the ingredients for a larger dessert.

1   (3-oz.) pkg. vanilla pudding mix (not instant)
1   cup milk
¾   cup amaretto-flavored nondairy liquid creamer
3   (½-inch thick) slices pound cake,
        cut in ½-inch pieces
3   tablespoons sherry
1½   (3½-oz.) pkg. dark chocolate truffles
1   (15½-oz.) can apricot halves, drained
1   cup whipping cream, whipped

1. In medium saucepan, combine pudding mix, milk and creamer. Cook according to pudding package directions. Remove from heat. Cover with parchment paper or plastic wrap to prevent skin from forming; refrigerate to cool completely.

2. Cover bottom of 1-quart serving bowl with cake pieces. Sprinkle with sherry. Coarsely chop 1 package truffles; spread over cake.

3. Reserve 3 apricot halves. With scissors, snip remaining apricots into strips; spoon over truffles. Pour cooled pudding over truffle pieces. Using a pastry bag and large star tip, cover surface with whipped cream rosettes, or spoon whipped cream over and rough surface with fork. Cut each of remaining truffles into triangles; insert into whipped cream. Garnish with strips of reserved apricots. Store in refrigerator until served. Refrigerate leftovers.

About 8 servings

Chocolate Truffle Trifle

Chocolate Truffle Trifle makes the perfect dessert dish for a morning or mid-day brunch—something sweet, with just the right amount of chocolate, yet it won't weigh you down.

Christmas Brunch

CHRISTMAS

Appetizer Buffet

MENU

ANTIPASTO SQUARES

WHITE BEAN SPREAD WITH ROSEMARY

CROSTINI

CAPONATA

CORNMEAL-PARMESAN BREADSTICKS

CHERRY TOMATOES FILLED
WITH PESTO CREAM CHEESE

ANISE-SCENTED PIZZELLE

The centerpiece of this menu is the Antipasto Squares—savory ricotta tarts topped with roasted red peppers and caramelized onions. Pesto-stuffed cherry tomatoes make attractive miniature pick-up hors d'oeuvres. For casual noshing, nothing beats garlicky bean spread, piquant eggplant caponata and cheesy breadsticks. And because it is the holidays, it seems appropriate to include a sweet: "different" but delicate pizzelle wafers add a final flourish to this wonderful holiday buffet.

Antipasto Squares with Roasted Red Pepper Topping and Carmelized Onion Topping

ANTIPASTO SQUARES

With a crisp pastry crust, herbed ricotta filling and toppings of roasted red peppers and caramelized onions, these squares resemble a savory cheesecake. Finishing the squares with 2 toppings creates an appealing variety, but you can simplify by using just one; if you choose the latter method, double topping proportions. (The toppings are also delicious served over crostini.) You don't need utensils to enjoy these squares, but it is a good idea to provide small plates.

Crust

   3 cups all-purpose flour
   1 teaspoon salt
   ¾ cup unsalted butter, cut into cubes
   ¼ cup extra-virgin olive oil
   1 egg
   2 teaspoons lemon juice
   ⅓ to ½ cup ice water

Filling

   1 egg
2 ½ cups part-skim ricotta cheese
   ½ cup freshly grated Parmesan cheese (2-oz.)
   ¼ cup chopped fresh parsley
   ¾ teaspoon dried oregano
   1 teaspoon salt
   ¼ teaspoon freshly ground pepper

Garnishes

  12 fresh Italian parsley leaves
   2 tablespoons chopped brine-cured black olives, such as kalamata

   1. To prepare crust, in large bowl, combine flour and salt. Using pastry blender or your fingertips, cut butter into flour mixture until it resembles fine crumbs with a few larger pieces. Drizzle in oil, stirring with fork until blended. In liquid measuring cup, beat egg and lemon juice lightly with fork. Stir in enough ice water to measure ⅔ cup. Gradually add just enough egg mixture to flour mixture, stirring briskly with a fork, until dough clumps together. Turn out onto lightly floured surface; knead several times, but do not overwork. Press dough into disk shape. Wrap in plastic wrap and

refrigerate at least 30 minutes. Dough can be prepared ahead. Refrigerate up to 4 days or freeze up to 2 months. Thaw frozen pastry in refrigerator. Let cold pastry stand at room temperature for 15 minutes before rolling.

2. Spray 15x10x1-inch jelly roll pan with nonstick cooking spray. On lightly floured surface, roll dough into rectangle slightly thinner than ¼-inch. Roll dough back over rolling pin, lift and unroll dough onto pan. Fit dough into edges of pan. With scissors, trim dough to extend ½-inch beyond pan rim. Fold edges under against pan rim and crimp. Prick bottom with fork. Cover with plastic wrap, chill 30 minutes or freeze 15 minutes. Meanwhile, heat oven to 400°F.

3. Line pastry shell with aluminum foil or parchment paper large enough to lift out easily. Spread pastry weights or dried beans evenly over bottom. Bake about 20 minutes or until firm. Carefully lift out foil and weights; return to oven and bake an additional 5 minutes or until very light golden. Let cool on rack. Reduce oven temperature to 350°F.

4. To make filling, in medium bowl, whisk egg and ricotta. Stir in Parmesan, parsley, oregano, salt and pepper. Spread over bottom of partially baked crust.

5. Bake tart 25 to 35 minutes or until filling is firm to the touch. Let cool in pan on wire rack. Tart base can be prepared ahead. Cover and refrigerate up to 8 hours.

6. Shortly before serving, with a serrated or sharp knife, cut tart into 24 squares. Arrange on platter(s). Spoon a generous tablespoon of Roasted Red Pepper Topping over 12 of the squares. Spoon a generous tablespoon Caramelized Onion Topping over remaining 12 squares. Garnish each caramelized onion square with a parsley leaf, then top with a sprinkling of chopped olives.

24 servings

ROASTED RED PEPPER TOPPING

2 red bell peppers
1 tablespoon extra-virgin olive oil
1 tablespoon red wine vinegar
1 tablespoon drained capers, rinsed
¼ teaspoon salt
¼ teaspoon freshly ground pepper

1. Heat broiler. Line baking sheet with aluminum foil. Cut peppers in half lengthwise and place, cut side down, on baking sheet. Broil 10 to 15 minutes or until peppers are blackened and blistered. Remove from broiler, cover with clean kitchen towel and let steam 10 to 20 minutes.

2. Slip skins off peppers; discard seeds. Halve peppers lengthwise, then cut crosswise into ¼-inch wide strips. Place in medium bowl. Add oil, vinegar, capers, salt and pepper; toss to mix. Topping can be prepared ahead. Cover and refrigerate up to 2 days.

1⅓ cups

CARAMELIZED ONION TOPPING

1 tablespoon olive oil
4 cups slivered onions
¼ teaspoon salt
2 teaspoons balsamic vinegar
¼ teaspoon freshly ground pepper

1. In large skillet, heat oil over medium heat until hot. Add onions and salt; cook, stirring frequently, 15 to 20 minutes or until very tender and lightly caramelized. (Reduce heat and add a little water, if necessary, to prevent scorching.) Remove from heat and stir in vinegar and pepper. Topping can be prepared ahead. Cover and refrigerate up to 2 days.

1⅓ cups

WHITE BEAN SPREAD WITH ROSEMARY

This easy spread is a useful addition to your repertoire of holiday recipes, because as long as you have a few basics on hand—canned beans, garlic and fresh rosemary—you can whip up an appetizer at a moment's notice. Even though the garlic is destined for the food processor, resist the temptation to dump in whole cloves. Mashing garlic into a paste with salt is the key to bringing out its mellow and rich, rather than harsh flavor.

4   medium garlic cloves, peeled, crushed
1   teaspoon kosher (coarse) salt
¼   teaspoon plus ⅛ teaspoon cayenne
2   (19-oz.) cans cannelini beans, drained, well-rinsed
⅓   cup extra-virgin olive oil
¼   cup fresh lemon juice
¼   teaspoon freshly ground pepper
1   tablespoon chopped fresh rosemary
1   teaspoon extra-virgin olive oil
2   sprigs fresh rosemary

1. Using mortar and pestle or with side of a chef's knife, mash garlic, salt and ¼ teaspoon of the cayenne into paste. In food processor, combine beans and garlic mixture; pulse into a chunky puree. Add ⅓ cup olive oil, lemon juice and freshly ground pepper; pulse just until mixed.

2. Transfer puree to medium bowl. Stir in chopped rosemary. Spread can be prepared ahead. Cover and refrigerate up to 2 days.

3. To serve, spoon into serving bowl(s), drizzle with 1 teaspoon olive oil, sprinkle with remaining cayenne, and garnish with rosemary sprigs.

24 servings

CROSTINI

Serve with the Caponata (page 11).

1   baguette
    Olive Oil cooking spray

1. Heat oven to 325°F. Cut baguette into ½-inch thick slices. Spray baking sheet with nonstick cooking spray. Arrange baguette slices in single layer on baking sheet. Lightly mist tops of baguette slices with cooking spray. Bake about 15 minutes or until crisp and very light golden. Crostini can be prepared ahead. Store in an airtight container up to 8 hours.

32 Crostini

ROUNDING OUT THE BUFFET

Supplement your homemade dishes by adding a few store-bought items.

❈ Bowls of Gaeta olives; a platter of prosciutto and Genoa salami; and a cheese tray featuring Italian cheeses such as Asiago, Gorgonzola and smoked mozzarella.

❈ A large bowl of winter fruits— such as pomegranates, grapes and tangerines—makes a lovely decoration, as well as a welcome snack.

❈ Of course, stock the bar with Italian wines. Wines that complement these bold-flavored foods include: crisp, dry Soave; sparkling Asto Spumate; and fruity Chianti Classico. Finally, don't forget to offer lots of sparkling water and nonalcoholic sparkling grape juice.

CAPONATA

This Sicilian relish is a useful holiday appetizer staple because it gets better as it sits. Serve the bowl
of Caponata surrounded by Crostini (page 130) and assorted crackers.

3 tablespoons olive oil
1 (1-lb.) eggplant, washed,
    cut into ½-inch cubes (6 cups)
1 cup chopped onion
1 cup finely diced celery ribs
4 medium garlic cloves, minced
⅛ teaspoon cayenne
1 (14½-oz.) can diced tomatoes, undrained
¼ cup sun-dried tomatoes, finely chopped
3 tablespoons red wine vinegar
8 Sicilian cracked green olives,
    pitted, chopped (⅓ cup)
2 tablespoons drained capers, rinsed
1 tablespoon sugar
3 tablespoons currants
¼ cup pine nuts, toasted (page 133)
3 tablespoons chopped fresh Italian parsley
3 sprigs fresh Italian parsley

1. In large skillet, heat 1 tablespoon oil over medium-high heat until hot. Add one-half of egg plant; cook, stirring and turning eggplant, 4 to 6 minutes or until browned and tender. Transfer to plate and set aside. Add another 1 tablespoon oil to skillet and repeat with remaining eggplant. Set aside.

2. Add remaining 1 tablespoon oil to skillet. Add onion and celery; cook, stirring often, 3 to 5 minutes or until softened. Add garlic and cayenne; cook, stirring constantly, 30 seconds. Add diced tomatoes, sun-dried tomatoes, vinegar, olives, capers, sugar and reserved eggplant; bring to a simmer. Reduce heat to medium-low, cover skillet and cook, stirring occasionally, about 15 minutes or until mixture has a chunky, jam-like consistency. Add currants and cook, covered, 1 minute. Remove from heat. Stir in pine nuts and chopped parsley. Let cool. Caponata can be prepared ahead. Cover and refrigerate up to 4 days. To serve, spoon into serving bowls; garnish with parsley sprigs.

32 (1-tablespoon) servings

CORNMEAL-PARMESAN BREADSTICKS

Homemade breadsticks are addictive, and they make great party food because they are easy to munch on without any worry about spills and drips. For an appealing presentation, stand these poppy-seed-flecked golden breadsticks upright in an attractive clay pot or vase.

2¼ to 2¾ cups all-purpose flour
1 cup yellow cornmeal
2 (¼-oz.) pkg. active dry yeast
2 teaspoons salt
1 teaspoon sugar
⅛ teaspoon cayenne
1⅓ cups water
2 tablespoons olive oil
1½ cups freshly grated Parmesan cheese (3½-oz.)
1 egg, beaten with 1 tablespoon water for glaze
¼ cup poppy seeds

1. In large mixing bowl, stir together 2¼ cups of the flour, cornmeal, yeast, salt, sugar and cayenne. In small saucepan, combine water and oil; heat over low heat until very warm (120°F to 130°F). Gradually pour hot liquid into flour mixture, beating with a wooden spoon or paddle attachment of stand-up mixer. Beat well. Stir in Parmesan and enough remaining flour until dough is too stiff to stir. Turn dough out onto lightly floured work surface and knead about 5 minutes, adding just enough flour to prevent sticking, until smooth.

Cover dough with plastic wrap and let rest 10 to 15 minutes.

2. Heat oven to 425°F. Spray 4 baking sheets with nonstick cooking spray or line with parchment paper. Divide dough into 4 pieces. (Keep any portions of dough you are not working with covered with plastic wrap.) On lightly floured surface, roll 1 piece into a ¼-inch-thick rough rectangle that measures about 12x8 inches. With pizza cutter or chef's knife, cut dough crosswise into 12 (1-inch wide) strips. Twist each strip into a straight coil; place on baking sheet. Brush breadsticks with egg glaze and sprinkle with poppy seeds.

3. Bake 15 to 20 minutes or until golden brown. Transfer to wire rack to cool. Repeat with remaining dough. Breadsticks can be baked in advance. Seal cooled breadsticks in plastic food storage bag and freeze up to 1 month. Shortly before serving, spread frozen breadsticks on baking sheet. Bake at 325°F 5 to 8 minutes.

48 breadsticks

CHERRY TOMATOES FILLED WITH PESTO CREAM CHEESE

Simply irresistible, these red-and-green bites are festive and elegant. The pesto cream cheese filling keeps well and can be prepared in advance, but wait until shortly before serving to stuff tomatoes. Cherry tomatoes lose their charm once they have been refrigerated. It is also a good idea to pick up fresh basil for garnish the day before or the day of the party. See these tomatoes pictured on page 124 and 126.

2 medium garlic cloves, peeled, crushed
1 teaspoon kosher (coarse) salt
3 cups fresh basil leaves, washed, dried
⅓ cup pine nuts, toasted
¼ teaspoon freshly ground pepper
1 tablespoon extra-virgin olive oil
1 (8-oz.) pkg. reduced-fat cream cheese (Neufchatel), cut into chunks
2 pints cherry tomatoes, washed, dried
2 cups fresh washed dried basil leaves
2 tablespoons pine nuts, toasted*

1. Using mortar and pestle or side of chef's knife, mash garlic and salt into paste. In food processor, combine basil, ⅓ cup pine nuts, pepper and mashed garlic; process until pine nuts are ground. With motor running, drizzle in olive oil. Add cream cheese; pulse until smooth and creamy. (Filling can be prepared ahead. Cover and refrigerate up to 2 days.)

2. Shortly before serving, with serrated or sharp paring knife, make an X on rounded side (opposite stem) of each cherry tomato. Using grapefruit spoon or your fingertips, scoop out seeds, taking care to keep tomatoes intact.

3. Spoon pesto cream cheese into pastry bag fitted with a star tip or small plastic food bag with a ½-inch hole snipped in one corner. Pipe rosette of filling into each cherry tomato cavity. Set each filled cherry tomato on basil leaf and arrange on serving platter. Garnish each one with toasted pine nut.

About 48 appetizers

☆ TIP

To toast pine nuts, in small skillet, toast pine nuts over medium-low heat, stirring constantly, 2 to 3 minutes or until light golden and fragrant. Transfer to small bowl and let cool.

ANISE-SCENTED PIZZELLE

Pizzelle, which are crisp Italian wafer cookies, add a delicate, sweet finish to an antipasto buffet and are a terrific addition to your holiday cookie jar. With their lacy, snowflake-like appearance, they have a festive air. For an elegant presentation, serve pizzelle on a tiered serving platter.

3 cups all-purpose flour
2 tablespoons anise seeds, crushed
¼ teaspoon salt
4 eggs
4 egg whites
1 ¼ cups sugar
1 cup butter, melted
¼ cup reduced-fat milk
2 tablespoons lemon juice
1 tablespoon vanilla
½ teaspoon anise extract
Powdered sugar for dusting

1. In medium bowl, whisk together flour, anise seeds and salt. In large bowl, beat egg, egg whites and sugar at high speed 5 to 7 minutes or until thickened and pale. Add butter, milk, lemon juice, vanilla and anise extract; beat at low speed until blended. Add flour mixture and beat at low speed just until incorporated. Do not overmix.

2. Heat pizzelle iron.* (If using a stovetop iron, heat over medium heat.) Spray lightly with cooking spray. Drop one generous tablespoon batter onto each pizzelle form. Close iron tightly to squeeze batter into thin layer. Bake about 1 minute or until light golden. With fork, transfer pizzelle to wire rack to cool. (If edges look a little ragged, trim with a paring knife while still hot.) Repeat with remaining batter, spraying iron with cooking spray as needed. Pizzelle will keep in an airtight container up to 1 week.

3. To serve, place an inverted 6-ounce custard cup or 4-inch circle of parchment paper over each pizzelle and dust with powdered sugar to make a decorative border around edges. Arrange on serving platter(s).

About 50 pizzelle

☆ TIP

Pizzelle are griddle-baked in a special pizzelle iron available in both stovetop and electric models (often made with convenient nonstick plate).

Christmas Appetizer Buffet

CHRISTMAS DINNER

with Game

by John Schumacher

Chef John Schumacher reflects: "Christmas for me brings fond memories of growing up on a small farm in western Minnesota. The dining room table sat 24 adults. As children, we sat around the kitchen table dreaming of the day when we could join the adults in the dining room. My mother used her own canned fruits and vegetables from the garden for Christmas dinner, as many farm families did. She served ducks or geese we hunted, or turkey we raised on our farm. Squash, potatoes, onions and carrots were brought up from the root cellar."

"For a special treat, my mother purchased pints of fresh oysters at the local farmer's store. The oysters smelled like salt and sand. We dreamed of far-off places like New England, but never dreamed we would ever see the ocean. Little did I know I would be a

CHRISTMAS DINNER

with Game

MENU

OYSTER BISQUE IN ROASTED ACORN SQUASH

SLOW-ROASTED DUCK

CORNBREAD STUFFING

BAKED YAMS WITH APPLE-PEAR COMPOTE

CHRISTMAS CHERRY MOUSSE

Serves 8

submarine sailor and spend some holidays under 200 feet of water!"

"This menu brings me back to a special time in my life. I now prepare Christmas dinner for my family in our country inn and everyone has to sit at the kids' table! These recipes use simple ingredients combined with love and holiday cheer to create life-long memories. Happy holidays!"

Chef John's Notes On Bisque and Squash:

- When slicing squash bottom, leave it thick enough so that soup won't drain out.
- Washing squash in acid water kills any bacteria on the outside of the squash.
- You can use whole milk or light cream instead of half-and-half.
- If you wish to prepare these 6 to 8 hours in advance, cool the hot base in the refrigerator well and then fill squash. Keep refrigerated until it is time to bake.
- This recipe is very adaptable. You may use shrimp, crab or sea legs, as well as mushrooms or other vegetables.
- Do not use raw fowl or red meat in this recipe.
- Make sure to keep each squash lid with its matching squash, for a proper seal during baking.

Oyster Bisque in Roasted Acorn Squash

8 medium-sized acorn squash
¼ cup vinegar
½ cup butter
½ cup shallots, cut into ¼-inch dice
⅓ cup flour
1 cup sherry wine
2 teaspoon salt
1 teaspoon nutmeg
1 teaspoon freshly ground pepper
2 pints light cream
2 pints fresh oysters, plus liquid
1 cup fresh mushrooms, cut into ¼-inch dice

1. Wash squash in cold water with vinegar. Remove squash from vinegar and pat dry. Place squash stem ends down on cutting board. If needed, trim bottoms to make squash stand straight.
2. With sharp paring knife, cut circle at 45-degree angle in top to make lid. Gently remove lid and scoop out seeds and pulp. In large saucepan, melt butter over medium-high heat. Add shallots and sauté until transparent. Add flour. Reduce heat to medium; cook 2 minutes, stirring constantly with wooden spoon to keep mixture from burning. Add sherry, salt, nutmeg and pepper, stirring gently to combine.
3. Remove from heat. Stir in half-and-half and oyster liquid. Heat oven to 375°F. Place squash bottoms in baking dish lined with aluminum foil. Place oyster and mushroom pieces into squash. Fill each squash with sherry mixture to the top. Cover with lid; bake 1 hour.

Serves 8

Oyster Bisque in Roasted Acorn Squash

This recipe brings the flavors of the farm together with fresh seafood. It is an attention-grabber to start the meal. Try shrimp, crab legs or sea legs, as well as mushroom and other vegetables in this very adaptable dish. (Do not use raw fowl or red meat.)

SLOW-ROASTED DUCK

This recipe is part of our traditional Christmas feast. The rich, dark meat presents the meal's dominant flavor.

4 (3-to 4-lb.) farm-raised ducks
½ cup salt
¼ cup lemon juice
4 large yellow onions, peeled
4 lemons
2 cup dry white wine
4 sprigs fresh rosemary

1. If ducks have skin on, remove all pin feathers and hairs. In sink filled half full of cold water, add salt and lemon juice. Let fowl stand in this solution 1 hour. Remove and rinse well, inside and out.

2. Heat oven to 275°F. In cavity of each duck, place one-half of whole onion. If using large ducks, place whole small lemon in each cavity. If using small wild ducks, place 2 whole lemons in each roasting bag.

3. Using 2 large plastic roasting bags, place 2 ducks in each bag, breast side up; add 1 cup white wine and 2 sprigs of rosemary to each bag. Cut 2-inch slit in top of each bag; place on roasting pan.

4. Bake 3 hours or until juices run clear and meat starts to separate from breast bone. Internal temperature must reach 180°F. Let fowl stand 10 to 15 minutes in bag while juices settle before carving. Remember that the larger the birds, the larger the bone and the longer it takes to roast or cook.

Serves 8

CORNBREAD STUFFING

*I am a firm believer in not stuffing fowl. I bake the stuffing in
a large Dutch oven. The flavor of sunflowers, honey and
cornmeal are just right to accompany fowl.*

½ cup olive oil
1½ cup red onions, cut into ¼-inch pieces
2 garlic cloves minced
1 cup celery, cut into ¼-inch slices
1 cup carrots, cut into ¼-inch pieces
1 cup yellow or red bell peppers,
    cut into ¼-inch pieces
½ cup sweet gherkin pickles, cut into ¼-inch pieces
6 cups cubed Honey-Sunflower Cornbread,
    cut into ½-inch cubes (recipe below)
3 eggs, beaten
1½ cups chicken stock
2 teaspoon dried thyme
1 teaspoon dried tarragon
1 teaspoon poultry seasoning
2 teaspoon Worcestershire sauce
½ teaspoon salt
½ teaspoon freshly ground pepper
1 cup fresh pears, peeled, cut into ½-inch pieces
1 cup dried prunes, cut into ½-inch pieces
1 cup green raisins

1. Heat oven to 350°F.

2. In large skillet, heat oil over medium-high heat until
   hot. Add onions, garlic, celery, carrots and bell
   peppers; sauté until onions are tender. Stir in
   pickles. Reduce heat to low; simmer 10 minutes.
   Place vegetables in large bowl. Stir in cornbread;
   toss to combine, being careful not to overmix.

3. In large bowl, whisk together eggs, chicken stock,
   thyme, tarragon, poultry seasoning, Worcestershire
   sauce, salt and pepper. Stir in pears, prunes, raisins
   and cornbread mixture. Place in Dutch oven or
   covered baking dish. Bake about 1 hour or until
   internal temperature reaches 160°F in center and
   stuffing is not watery.

Serves 8

CORNBREAD STUFFING VARIATIONS

* Maryland style: Add 2 cups raw oysters
  and liquid in last step. Very gently fold
  into stuffing.

* Southwestern style: Add seeded hot chile
  peppers cut into ¼-inch cubes.

* Heartland style: Add 1 cup pork sausage
  with vegetables in first step.

* Canadian style: Add 1½ cups smoked
  salmon pieces in last step.

HONEY-SUNFLOWER CORNBREAD

For use in Cornbread Stuffing.

1 cup half-and-half
2 eggs, beaten
¼ cup honey
¼ cup vegetable oil
¼ cup packed brown sugar
½ teaspoon salt
1 cup all-purpose flour
1 cup yellow cornmeal
1 tablespoon baking powder
½ cup unsalted sunflower seeds

1. Heat oven to 375°F. Spray 9-inch square pan with
   nonstick cooking spray.

2. In bowl, whisk together half-and-half, eggs, honey,
   vegetable oil, brown sugar and salt. In another bowl,
   combine flour, cornmeal, baking powder and
   sunflower seeds. Stir dry ingredients into wet
   ingredients just until combined and moistened.
   Pour into pan. Bake 20 to 25 minutes or until
   toothpick inserted in center comes out clean.

BAKED YAMS WITH APPLE-PEAR COMPOTE

*Yams and sweet potatoes in my youth were only prepared for Thanksgiving and Christmas dinners. This recipe
contains roasted yams with the flavor of apples, pears and pecans (our special holiday nuts).*

Apple-Pear Compote

2   tablespoon butter
½   cup red onions, cut into ¼-inch pieces
2   cups tart apples, peeled, cut into ½-inch pieces
2   cups Bartlett pears, cut into ¼-inch pieces
½   cup packed brown sugar
1   teaspoon cornstarch
1   teaspoon salt
1   teaspoon ground nutmeg
1   teaspoon ground cinnamon
1   tablespoon fresh lemon juice
     ½ cup dark rum or cranberry juice
½   cup pecan pieces

Brown Sugar-Pecan Topping

½   cup packed brown sugar
½   cup pecan pieces
½   teaspoon ground nutmeg
⅛   teaspoon Cajun pepper

8   yams

1. To prepare compote, in large skillet, heat butter over
    medium-high heat until melted. Add onions; sauté
    until just tender. Stir in apples and pears; reduce
    heat to medium. Simmer 2 minutes,
    stirring frequently.

2. In small bowl, combine brown sugar, cornstarch,
    salt, nutmeg and cinnamon. Sprinkle over fruit. Stir

in lemon juice and rum; simmer over low heat
10 minutes, stirring frequently to keep from
burning. Remove from heat. Stir in pecan pieces.
Cool; store covered in refrigerator.

3. To prepare topping, place brown sugar, pecans,
    nutmeg and pepper in heavy-duty resealable plastic
    bag; lightly pound with meat mallet until mixture is
    finely ground.

4. Heat oven to 350°F. Wash yams, brushing skins
    with stiff vegetable brush. Place flat-side down on
    baking sheet, making sure you have room on all
    sides to let heat circulate. Pierce yams to allow
    steam to escape. Bake 50 minutes or until tender.
    Cool 10 minutes.

5. Slice ½-inch-thick piece off top of each yam.
    Remove pulp from skin; place in large bowl. With
    teaspoon, scoop out center, leaving ½-inch shell.
    Pour liquid from compote into yam pulp; mash
    with hand-held potato masher until smooth. Add
    compote to yam pulp mixture; fold
    to distribute well.

6. Fill each yam shell. Bake 20 minutes. Sprinkle each
    yam with topping. Return to oven and bake an
    additional 5 minutes.

Serves 8

CHRISTMAS CHERRY MOUSSE

Of course, as children we did not call this holiday dessert "mousse." We simply called it Christmas Pudding with Cherries and Whipped Cream.

Christmas Cherry Mousse
    Cream Pie Filling (recipe follows)
    Vanilla Whipped Cream (recipe follows)
6 cups whole red cherries, frozen
    Coconut Topping (recipe follows)
8 small candy canes

Cream Pie Filling
10 cups milk
12 egg yolks
1½ cups plus 4 tablespoons cornstarch
3½ cups sugar
4 teaspoons vanilla
⅛ teaspoon salt
2 tablespoons butter

Vanilla Sugar
3 cups granulated sugar
3 whole vanilla beans

Vanilla Whipped Cream
2 pints extra-heavy whipping cream
½ cup Vanilla Sugar (Recipe above)
2 teaspoons vanilla

Coconut Topping
2 cups shredded coconut
¼ cup Vanilla Sugar
¼ cup créme de menthe

1. To prepare Cream Pie Filling, in large saucepan, simmer 9 cups of the milk. In blender, mix remaining 1 cup milk, egg yolks, cornstarch, sugar, vanilla and salt 30 seconds. Add mixture to hot milk; stir constantly until thickened. Add butter. Transfer mixture to glass bowl; refrigerate.

2. To prepare Vanilla Sugar for use in Vanilla Whipped Cream, combine sugar and vanilla beans in tightly covered jar; let sit 2 days.

3. To prepare Vanilla Whipped Cream, in chilled large bowl, combine whipping cream, ½ cup Vanilla Sugar (prepared above) and 2 teaspoons vanilla; beat at high speed until stiff peaks form. Cover; refrigerate until ready to use.

4. To prepare Coconut Topping, preheat oven to 300°F. In large resealable bag, combine shredded coconut and sugar; toss to combine. Add créme de menthe; toss well. Place mixture on aluminum-foil lined baking sheet. Bake 15 minutes at 300°F. Remove from oven; toss and let cool in pan. Store in covered jar until ready to use.

5. To create Christmas Cherry Mousse Filling, place one-half of the Cream Pie Filling in large chilled bowl. Add ½ cup liquid from frozen cherries; whisk until smooth. Add 2 cups Vanilla Whipped Cream; gently fold in with wire whisk.

6. To assemble Christmas Cherry Mousse, gather 8 tall-stemmed glasses. Place 2 or 3 cherries in bottom of glass. Top with layer of Vanilla Whipped Cream about 1 inch thick. Add layer of Cherry Mousse filling; add 3 cherries. Add second layer of Vanilla Whipped Cream, cherry mousse filling and 3 cherries. Top with dollop of Vanilla Whipped Cream. Sprinkle with coconut topping; place candy cane down center of each glass.

Serves 8

Christmas Cherry Mousse

DESSERT

Buffet

by Lisa Golden Schroeder

DESSERT
Buffet

MENU

HOLIDAY JEWEL TART

TUXEDO TRUFFLES

COCONUT-CARAMEL CHEESECAKE
WITH TROPICAL FRUIT

RUM-SOAKED GINGER BUNDT CAKE

ORANGE MASCARPONE FONDUE

PISTACHIO-MINT BROWNIES

Serves 10-12

There is nothing more indulgent and fun than offering an array of lovely desserts to family and friends. Many of the following recipes can be made ahead, but there are always great options for filling out a buffet if you don't have time to prepare them all.

A dessert condiment bar (set up next to the desserts, coffee and other hot beverages) could include small bowls of softly whipped cream, grated sweet chocolate, coarsely ground espresso beans, chocolate-covered coffee beans or after-dinner mints. Small shakers of

ground nutmeg, cinnamon and vanilla powder create the atmosphere of an intimate café latte shop. Any of these condiments could be spooned or sprinkled onto desserts or into hot beverages.

No matter what you choose to make, from Pistachio-Mint Brownies or Tuxedo Truffles to a decadent Coconut Caramel Cheesecake, a dessert buffet is a wonderful and very welcome way to entertain during the holidays.

Dessert Buffet

HOLIDAY JEWEL TART

Choose the type of chocolate and dried fruit you like best in this simple tart. Try dark chocolate and dried cherries or white chocolate and dried cranberries—any combination will win! Make the tart up to two days ahead and store at room temperature.

Crust
- 1 cup all-purpose flour
- 3 tablespoons sugar
- ½ cup butter
- 1 egg yolk
- ¼ teaspoon almond extract

Filling
- 1 cup sugar
- ¼ cup butter, melted
- 2 eggs
- 2 teaspoons vanilla
- ½ cup all-purpose flour
- 1 cup coarsely chopped semisweet or white chocolate (6-oz.)
- ½ cup dried cherries or cranberries
- ¼ cup golden raisins
- ¼ cup toasted chopped almonds

1. Heat oven to 350°F. In food processor, combine flour, sugar, butter, egg and almond; process just until dough forms. Press dough in bottom and up sides of 9 or 10-inch tart pan with removable bottom. Place pan on baking sheet; refrigerate.

2. In medium bowl, combine 1 cup sugar, butter, eggs and vanilla; mix well. Stir in ½ cup flour until well blended. Add chocolate, cherries or cranberries, raisins and almonds, stirring just to combine.

3. Pour filling into pastry-lined pan. Bake 45 to 50 minutes or until top of tart is crusty and deep golden brown, and tip of knife inserted in center comes out clean.

4. Cool tart completely on wire rack. Cover; store at room temperature until serving time.

10 servings

TUXEDO TRUFFLES

No dessert table is complete without something terribly chocolatey. Truffles are uniquely suited to fill this requirement! A traditional ganache filling is chocolate and cream, but here chocolate-hazelnut spread (Nutella is the best known brand) adds great flavor and a creamy texture. The filling will set up more quickly than many truffle fillings, so dipping can be done sooner. These are truly elegant tuxedo candies—the centers are dipped into white chocolate first, then drizzled with dark chocolate.

Filling
- 1¼ cups semisweet chocolate, chopped (8-oz.)
- ¼ cup chocolate-hazelnut spread, such as Nutella
- ¼ cup whipping cream

Coatings
- 1¼ cups white chocolate, chopped (8-oz.)
- ¾ cups semisweet chocolate, chopped* (4-oz.)

1. Place 8-oz. chocolate and chocolate-hazelnut spread in small bowl. In small saucepan, heat cream until nearly boiling. Pour over chocolate mixture. Whisk until chocolate is melted and filling is smooth.

2. Cover bowl with plastic wrap; refrigerate filling 15 to 20 minutes or until firm enough to scoop.

3. Line rimmed baking sheet with parchment paper. Scoop filling with tablespoon. Roll into 1-inch balls; place on baking sheet. Refrigerate 30 minutes or until very firm.

4. Meanwhile, place white chocolate in medium bowl set on top of smaller saucepan filled halfway with water (bottom of bowl should not touch water or rest on bottom of saucepan). Bring water to a boil; reduce heat so water is just simmering. Stir white chocolate until melted. Keep warm over barely simmering water. Using a fork, dip truffles into melted white chocolate to coat. Place on baking sheets; refrigerate until chocolate is set.

2 dozen truffles

*TRUFFLE TIPS

Melt truffle 4 oz. chocolate in another bowl over simmering water (or in microwave). Dip tines of fork into melted chocolate; drizzle over truffles. Store in airtight container in refrigerator. Serve at room temperature.

Holiday Jewel Tart

Tuxedo Truffles

Dessert Buffet

Coconut-Carmel Cheesecake with Tropical Fruit

COFFEE AND OTHER HOT BEVERAGE SUGGESTIONS

For many people, dessert is not complete without a steaming cup of coffee, espresso or cappuccino. Coffee carafes or an urn (large urns can be rented at party rental stores) can be filled with coffee, spiced chai or cranberry teas, or even hot chocolate. If you're lucky enough to have an espresso maker, you can offer beverages with steamed milk. Don't forget that pitchers of chilled or hot eggnog are always a favorite this time of year. Flavor eggnog with coffee or chocolate syrup for a change of pace.

If you offer coffee, your dessert condiment bar could be set up near the coffee carafes. Invest in a selection of Italian coffee syrups, found in the coffee section of the grocery store or specialty shops, for guests to

individually flavor their libations. Several brands of syrups are available, some with beautifully shaped bottles and elegant labels. Hazelnut, caramel, raspberry and almond are among the multitude of flavors you could offer. Liqueurs, too, have a place here—créme de menthe, Grand Marnier, amaretto, and Frangelico are decadent additions to any hot beverage.

Have an assortment of barware and mugs available for your guests. Large latte cups, tiny demitasse or Irish coffee mugs all make enticing presentations.

COCONUT-CARAMEL CHEESECAKE WITH TROPICAL FRUIT

Unsweetened coconut milk is often the base for Asian entrées and curry dishes. This dense, creamy cheesecake uses cream of coconut—a sweetened coconut mixture that is known as an ingredient in piña coladas and is found in the beverage aisle of the grocery. Baking the cheesecake in a water bath ensures even baking and can also prevent the top from cracking.

To serve this cheesecake on a buffet, drizzle with some caramel sauce, then garnish the top with some fresh fruit and coconut. Serve additional sauce and fruit on the side, or create a fruit salsa with chopped strawberries, fresh pineapple, kiwi and papaya to spoon over each slice. Using a knife dipped in hot water makes slicing the cake easier.

Crust
- ½ cup coarsely chopped macadamia nuts
- 2 tablespoons sugar
- 1½ cups crushed crisp coconut macaroon cookies (about eight 2½-inch cookies)
- ¼ cup butter, melted

Filling
- 3 (8-oz.) pkg. cream cheese, softened
- ½ cup cream of coconut
- ½ cup sour cream
- ¼ cup packed brown sugar
- 3 eggs
- ½ teaspoon coconut extract
- ½ teaspoon vanilla

Caramel Sauce
- 1 cup sugar
- ¾ cup water
- ½ cup whipping cream

  Assorted sliced tropical fruit (starfruit, kumquats, mango, papaya, kiwi)
  Toasted shaved coconut, if desired

1. Heat oven to 350°F. In food processor, process macadamia nuts and sugar until nuts are finely ground. Add cookie crumbs; pulse several times to combine. Transfer mixture to medium bowl; stir in butter until mixture is completely moistened. Press crust mixture evenly onto bottom and 1½ inches up side of 9-inch springform pan. Wrap outside of pan with a double layer of aluminum foil. (Set pan on top of foil and fold foil up around base of pan.)*

2. In large bowl, beat cream cheese, cream of coconut, sour cream and brown sugar at low speed until very smooth. Beat in eggs, one at a time, until well blended. Add coconut extract and vanilla; beat just until blended.

3. Pour filling into springform pan. Place springform pan in large, shallow roasting pan; pour 1-inch hot water into larger pan. Place pans in oven. Bake 60 minutes or until top is golden brown and filling stills jiggles a little. Turn off oven without opening door; let cake cool 1 hour. Transfer cake to wire rack; cool about 1 hour or until room temperature. Cover pan with plastic wrap; refrigerate at least 6 hours or overnight.

4. To serve, release cake from springform pan. Serve with Caramel Sauce, tropical fruit and toasted shaved coconut.

5. To prepare Caramel Sauce, in 2-quart saucepan, combine sugar and water. Cook over medium-low heat without stirring about 12 minutes or until sugar is completely dissolved and mixture begins to boil. Wash down sugar crystals from sides of pan with wet brush. Increase heat to high. Boil mixture, uncovered, 9 to 11 minutes or until syrup is deep golden brown.

6. Remove from heat. Carefully stir in cream (it will splatter). Return to low heat and stir until smooth. Serve warm. If prepared ahead, reheat until smooth and pourable. Store leftovers in refrigerator.

12 servings

✼ TIP
Cheesecake may be baked in a 9-inch round cake pan. Line pan with foil, leaving at least 3 inches overhanging edges of pan; press in crust and fill as directed above. Once baked and refrigerated, the cheesecake can be lifted from the pan using the foil.

Dessert Buffet

Rum-Soaked Ginger Bundt Cake

RUM-SOAKED GINGER BUNDT CAKE

Bundt cake pans come in many sizes and shapes—a star-shaped Bundt would have a place at the holiday buffet. Plan on preparing the cake at least one day ahead, as it needs time to soak up a rum syrup that is poured over the warm cake. Be sure to grate enough orange peel for both the cake and the Ginger Créme topping.

Ginger Cake

½	cup chopped pecans or walnuts
2½	cups all-purpose flour
2	tablespoons chopped crystallized ginger
2	teaspoons ground ginger
1	teaspoon cinnamon
½	teaspoon ground allspice
1	teaspoon baking soda
½	teaspoon salt
½	cup butter, softened
⅓	cup packed brown sugar
1	cup light molasses
2	eggs
1	tablespoon grated orange peel
1	cup buttermilk

Rum Syrup

⅓	cup sugar
¼	cup orange juice
2	tablespoons butter
½	cup dark rum
	Ginger Créme

Ginger Créme

1½	cups whipping cream
2	tablespoons packed brown sugar
1	tablespoon finely chopped crystallized ginger
1	teaspoon grated orange peel

1. Heat oven to 325°F. Spray 12-cup Bundt pan with nonstick cooking spray; lightly flour. Sprinkle nuts evenly in bottom of pan. In medium bowl, combine flour, crystallized and ground gingers, cinnamon, allspice, baking soda and salt; set aside.

2. In large bowl, beat butter and brown sugar at medium speed 2 to 3 minutes or until light and creamy. Add molasses, eggs and orange peel; beat 1 minute.

3. Add flour mixture and buttermilk alternately to butter mixture, beating at low speed after each addition, just until combined. Pour batter into pan.

4. Bake 50 minutes or until toothpick inserted in center comes out clean. Cool cake on wire rack 10 minutes; remove from pan onto aluminum foil-lined baking sheet.

5. Meanwhile, prepare rum syrup. Combine sugar, orange juice and butter in small sauce pan; bring to a boil. Remove from heat; stir in rum.

6. Poke warm cake thoroughly with toothpick or wooden skewer. Spoon warm Rum Syrup slowly over top, allowing it to be absorbed. Wrap cake in foil; let stand at least 24 hours. Serve with Ginger Créme Topping.

7. To prepare Ginger Créme Topping, in large bowl, combine cream and sugar; beat at high speed until soft peaks form. Stir in crystallized ginger and orange peel. Refrigerate until ready to serve.

12 servings

TRY SOME CHEESE

Rich cheese courses are making a huge comeback in restaurants, and are generally offered before dessert or in place of it. Offer a few creamy cheeses such as Camembert, Brie, Pont L'Eveque or fresh goat cheese drizzled with honey, along with wholemeal biscuits, toasted nut bread and perhaps some grapes. A selection of dessert wines, such as moscato d'Asti or tawny port would be a lovely accompaniment. A dessert cheese and wine tasting could make a great party by itself! The Orange Mascarpone Fondue (page 153) banks on combining both elements.

ORANGE MASCARPONE FONDUE

Deeply-flavored dessert wines are enjoying a surge in popularity. By concentrating the natural grape sugars found in sweet wines, it's possible to reduce the amount of processed sugar used in desserts and add another dimension of fruit flavor to dessert sauces and other dishes. Here, orange Muscat wine, made from very ripe Muscat grapes, can be found at wine shops, along with other dessert wines. You could also try a framboise (raspberry) wine or late-harvest Riesling. Mascarpone is a creamy, mild fresh Italian cheese that combines well with the wine.

1½ cups orange Muscat wine (Essensia or other Muscat wine) or ¼ cup orange juice concentrate and ¼ cup water
2 cups (16 oz.) mascarpone cheese
¼ teaspoon grated lemon peel
4 cups (1-inch) pound cake cubes
    Sliced fresh fruit
        (Asian pears, apples, Bosc or red pears)
    Biscotti, thin ginger cookies or toasted
        sliced raisin-walnut bread, if desired

1. Heat oven to 450°F. Spread cake cubes on rimmed baking sheet; bake 5 to 7 minutes or until lightly toasted.

2. In small saucepan, boil wine 12 to 14 minutes until reduced to ½ cup. If using orange juice concentrate, just combine with water; do not reduce.

3. Reduce heat to medium-high; add cheese and lemon peel. Stir about 4 minutes or until boiling. Set pan on warming tray or pour into small fondue pan set over candle.

4. Arrange cake cubes, fruit and other dippers on large platter. Use forks or long wood skewers to spear cake or fruit to dip in fondue.

10 servings

PISTACHIO-MINT BROWNIES

Childhood memories of gooey brownies come to life in these elegant wedges. Filled with mint-chocolate after-dinner mints, and simply glazed, a sprinkle of chopped pistachios is the perfect final touch.

Brownies
½ cup butter
1 cup unsweetened chocolate, chopped (3-oz.)
1 cup sugar
2 eggs
1 teaspoon vanilla
½ cup all-purpose flour
½ cup coarsely chopped crème de menthe thin mints (16 mints)
½ cup plus ⅓ cup chopped pistachio nuts

Chocolate-Mint Glaze
1 cup semisweet chocolate,
    chopped or chocolate chips (6-oz.)
⅓ cup whipping cream
⅛ teaspoon mint extract

1. Heat oven to 350°F. Line 8 or 9-inch square pan with aluminum foil, leaving an overhang to help lift cooled brownies from pan. Spray bottom of pan with nonstick cooking spray.

2. In medium saucepan, melt butter and chocolate over low heat, stirring frequently. Remove from heat; stir in sugar, eggs, vanilla, flour, mints and ½ cup of the pistachios.

3. Spread batter evenly in pan. Bake 25 to 30 minutes or until edges feel firm to touch and begin to turn a shade darker. Cool on wire rack.

4. Lift cooled brownies from pan; peel away foil from sides. Spread top of brownies with warm glaze. Sprinkle with remaining ⅓ cup pistachios. Let stand until glaze is set. Cut brownies into 9 squares, then cut each square in half diagonally.

5. To prepare Chocolate-Mint Glaze, in small saucepan, combine chocolate and cream. Cook and stir over low heat until chocolate is melted and mixture is smooth. Remove from heat; stir in mint extract.

18 brownies

Dessert Buffet

NEW YEAR'S EVE
for Two
by Mary Evans

New Year's Eve

for Two

Menu

Avocado and
Smoked Salmon Crostini

Stilton and
Walnut Salad

Individual
Potatoes Anna

Beef Tenderloin
in Port Wine-Pepper Sauce

Molten Chocolate Cakes

Serves 2

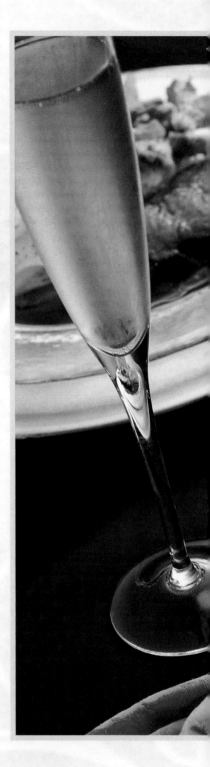

There are many ways to usher in the New Year, but one of the best has to be a romantic and luxurious dinner for two. Combining the flavors of the sea (Salmon Crostini), garden and forest (Stilton and Walnut Salad and Potatoes Anna) and prairie (Beef Tenderloin)...this meal does the job in classic fashion.

Add a roaring fire, fine wine and your favorite companion for the perfect celebration. Take all evening to enjoy—you only have to finish in time to toast the New Year in blissful contentment.

New Year's Eve for Two

Avocado and Smoked Salmon Crostini

AVOCADO AND SMOKED SALMON CROSTINI

Purchase the best smoked salmon available for this flavorful appetizer. Look for avocados that yield lightly when pressed. If necessary, purchase avocados several days in advance and allow to ripen at room temperature.

8 (¼-inch-thick) slices stale French bread
    (or diagonally-cut slices baguette)
¼ avocado, diced (¼-inch thick)
1½ teaspoons lemon juice
1 oz. lox-style sliced smoked salmon,
    diced (¼-inch thick)
¼ cup créme fraîche or cream cheese
1 tablespoon minced chives
⅛ teaspoon freshly ground pepper

1. Heat oven to 350°F. On baking sheet, bake bread slices 10 minutes or until dry and crispy. Remove; cool.

2. In small bowl, toss avocado with lemon juice. Gently stir diced salmon into avocado. Cover; refrigerate until ready to serve.

3. In small bowl, stir together créme fraîche, chives and pepper. Cover; refrigerate until ready to serve. Spread bread with créme fraîche mixture; top with avocado and salmon mixture.

2 servings

158

STILTON AND WALNUT SALAD

Stilton is Britain's most famous blue cheese. Substitute another flavorful variety if Stilton is unavailable.

1   tablespoon mayonnaise
1   tablespoon champagne or white wine vinegar
2   tablespoons vegetable oil
3   cups bite-size pieces romaine lettuce
¼   cup crumbled Stilton cheese
¼   cup walnut halves

I. Whisk together mayonnaise and vinegar in small bowl. Slowly whisk in oil. Just before serving, toss romaine with dressing and cheese; divide between two chilled salad plates. Sprinkle with walnut halves.

2 servings

INDIVIDUAL POTATOES ANNA

Use water chestnut or bamboo shoot cans, with tops and bottoms removed, for the rings. When inverted to unmold, the potatoes' crispy brown bottom makes them attractive for serving.

3   tablespoons melted butter
¾   pound Idaho russet potatoes, peeled, thinly sliced
½   teaspoon salt
⅛   teaspoon freshly ground pepper

I. Heat oven to 425°F. Wrap aluminum foil around outside and bottom of 2 (3¼-inch) rings. Place on baking sheet. Brush inside of rings and foil with melted butter.

2. Place single layer of potatoes over buttered foil bottom. Brush potatoes with butter; sprinkle with salt and pepper. Continue layering potatoes; brushing with butter and sprinkling with salt and pepper. Drizzle any remaining butter over top layer.

3. Bake 30 minutes or until potatoes are tender when pierced with knife. Loosen edges with tip of knife; invert onto dinner plates; remove rings and foil.

2 servings

WHICH CHAMPAGNE?

Effervescent wines are made all over the world from many different grapes and by many different methods. But they're not all Champagne. The French zealously protect the name "Champagne," insisting that the only true Champagnes come from the Champagne region in northeastern France. Many wine professionals respect that distinction and call everything else "sparkling wine." In pratice, the two terms are often used interchangeably, and you will see Champagne used as a generic term on wine that does not come from France.

For cooking, select a drinkable, moderately priced sparkling wine. Inexpensive sparkling wines can be unpleasantly sweet and sometimes bitter and metallic. When the wine is reduced during cooking, these disagreeable qualities become even more apparent. And it would be heresy to cook with a high-priced fine Champagne (unless you happen to have an open leftover bottle). These wines are far too elegant for the cooking pot and should be savored just as they are.

For most savory dishes, non-vintage brut (dry) sparkling wine is the best choice. You can use a brut wine for a dessert recipe, but a sweeter demi-sec (half-dry, or sweet) also works very well (look for *semi-seco* on Spanish bottles). Much of the sparkling Asti imported from Italy is quite sweet, so it's another good choice for dessert. Most of the sparkling wine on the merchant's shelf is non-vintage; it's had all the aging it's going to get, and it's ready to open and serve. You should have no trouble finding a satisfactory wine in the $7 to $15 range.

Individual Potatoes Anna, Beef Tenderloin in Port Wine-Pepper Sauce, Stilton and Walnut Salad

BEEF TENDERLOIN IN PORT WINE-PEPPER SAUCE

Allowing the tenderloins to rest while preparing the sauce lets the interior juices move toward the more well-done exterior, giving the steak a more even, medium-rare appearance.

2   tablespoons vegetable oil
2   (6-oz.) beef tenderloins, flattened to
        about 1½-inch thickness
⅛   teaspoon salt
⅛   teaspoon freshly ground pepper
2   tablespoons minced shallots
⅓   cup Port wine
2   teaspoons tomato paste
½   teaspoon freshly ground pepper
⅓   cup plus 2 teaspoons canned beef broth
¾   teaspoon cornstarch

I. In medium skillet, heat 1 tablespoon of the oil over medium-high heat until hot. Season steaks with salt and pepper; cook about 8 to 10 minutes, turning occasionally, until medium-rare. Remove to warm plate; cover lightly with foil.

2. In same skillet, add remaining 1 tablespoon oil and shallots. Reduce heat to medium; cook 2 to 3 minutes or until slightly softened. Add Port, tomato paste and pepper; increase heat to high and cook 3 to 4 minutes or until reduced by half. Add ⅓ cup beef broth; cook 1 to 2 minutes or until reduced slightly.

3. In small bowl, stir remaining 2 teaspoons beef broth and cornstarch together. Stir into wine mixture; cook about 30 seconds or until thickened. Spoon pool of sauce on dinner plate; top with steak and drizzle small amount of sauce over top.

2 servings

Molten Chocolate Cakes

These intensely chocolate cakes can be prepared a day ahead and baked at the last minute. The outside bakes into cake while the center turns to soft and luscious chocolate.

Center

1 oz. bittersweet chocolate, chopped
1 tablespoon orange juice
1 tablespoon orange liqueur

Cake

½ cup bittersweet chocolate, chopped (3-oz.)
2 tablespoons unsalted butter
1 tablespoon orange juice
1 tablespoon orange liqueur
1 egg
1 egg yolk
3 tablespoons sugar
3 tablespoons all-purpose flour

1. In small microwave-safe bowl, combine 1 oz. chocolate, 1 tablespoon orange juice and 1 tablespoon orange liqueur. Microwave on medium 1 minute or until softened. Stir until smooth. Line 2 ice cube tray cavities with plastic wrap. Spoon melted chocolate mixture into cavities. Freeze several hours or overnight.

2. Heat oven to 425°F. Generously butter 2 (6-oz.) custard cups. Line bottom of each cup with parchment paper; lightly butter each sheet of paper.

3. In small microwave-safe bowl, combine ½ cup chocolate, butter, 1 tablespoon orange juice and 1 tablespoon orange liqueur. Microwave on medium about 1½ minutes or until softened. Stir until smooth; cool to room temperature.

4. In medium bowl, beat egg and egg yolk at medium speed until blended. Slowly add sugar; beat 4 to 5 minutes at high speed or until egg mixture has tripled in volume and is light and fluffy. Fold in chocolate mixture. Fold in flour. Pour mixture into custard cups. Batter can be prepared up to 24 hours ahead. Cover and refrigerate custard cups at this point. Let stand at room temperature 30 minutes before baking.

5. Remove plastic wrap from frozen chocolate cubes. Remove small amount of cake batter from center of each custard cup. Push frozen cube down slightly into batter. Replace batter; spread over cube. Place custard cups on baking sheet; bake on center oven rack 14 to 18 minutes or until puffed and firm to the touch. Invert each cake onto serving plate, loosening sides with thin knife blade, if necessary. Peel off parchment paper; serve immediately with sweetened whipped cream.

2 servings

Choosing Champagne

Champagne is the perfect start and finish to this elegant meal. Choose a good quality imported French Champagne or a domestic sparkling wine made using the traditional Champagne method. Choose brut Champagne, the driest variety made. For the main course, look for a red wine without too much tanin, but with enough body to stand up to the pepper in the dish. Try a reputable California Merlot or a French Côte du Rhone-Villages. Dessert is best served with coffee. Return to Champagne for your New Year's toast.

New Year's Eve for Two

162

Family

NEW YEAR'S EVE

by Lisa Golden Schroeder

Breakfast for supper...a novel meal reversal that always seems to tickle kids and satisfy adults. This menu is reminiscent of pancake supper fundraisers—but a lot more fun and interesting. This menu is perfect for holding a New Year's Eve celebration for the entire family: safe and cozy at home, anticipating the new year.

Get everyone involved—stirring pancake batter, slicing fruit and flipping supper cakes. Most of the toppings, especially the Creamy Mushroom-Onion Sauce and Pizza Sauté, can be easily prepared ahead, then finished or rewarmed before serving. Remember the

Family
NEW YEAR'S EVE

MENU

SAVORY CORNMEAL SUPPER CAKES

WITH

MAPLE HARVEST HAM SAUTE

OR

CREAMY MUSHROOM-ONION SAUCE

OR

PIZZA SAUTE

VEGETABLE SLAW WITH MINT

RASPBERRY-ALMOND
FUDGE PARFAITS

Serves 4

sparkling grape juice, along with the Champagne. Put noisemakers and hats on your shopping list too.

Once the tummies are filled and a little clean-up done but the evening still young, relax awhile. Introduce younger family members to favorite old movies, a great board game or music that everyone can dance to... and savor luscious Raspberry-Almond Fudge Parfaits together. Midnight won't be far away.

SAVORY CORNMEAL SUPPER CAKES

In addition to the toppings given below, consider including bowls of shredded or crumbled cheeses (such as Parmesan or feta), a plain cheddar cheese sauce, sour cream, herb butters or even maple and berry syrups to drizzle over these tender cakes. These cakes are fragrant with green onion, and meld well with both savory and sweet toppings.

I cup yellow cornmeal
⅔ cup all-purpose flour
I teaspoon baking powder
I teaspoon baking soda
I teaspoon sugar
¼ teaspoon salt
I egg
1⅔ cup buttermilk
½ cup sliced green onions
I tablespoon olive oil

1. In medium bowl, mix cornmeal, flour, baking powder, baking soda, sugar and salt. Whisk in egg and buttermilk until batter is smooth. Stir in onions and oil.

2. Place griddle or large skillet over medium heat. When hot, spoon ¼ cup batter onto griddle. Cook until edges look dry; turn with wide spatula and cook 3 to 4 minutes or until golden brown.

3. Keep pancakes warm on baking sheet in warm oven. Serve with toppings (recipes follow).

4 to 6 servings

Savory Cornmeal Supper Cakes

SUPPER CAKE TOPPINGS

Maple Harvest Ham Sauté
I tablespoon butter
2 large pears or apples, thinly sliced
¾ cup maple syrup
12 oz. sliced Canadian bacon or ham, cut into narrow strips

1. In large skillet, melt butter over medium heat. Add pears; sauté 4 minutes or until nearly tender. Stir in maple syrup and ham; cook and stir an additional 2 minutes. Serve hot over pancakes.

4 cups

Creamy Mushroom-Onion Sauce

½ oz. dried mushroom pieces
1 tablespoon olive oil
1 onion, halved, thinly sliced
1 tablespoon tomato paste
8 oz. button mushrooms, sliced
8 oz. wild mushrooms
    (shiitake, crimini, chanterelle), sliced
2 tablespoons all-purpose flour
¾ cup low-fat milk
3 tablespoons finely chopped fresh dill
    or 1 teaspoon dried dillweed
1½ teaspoons garlic salt
½ teaspoon freshly ground pepper
½ cup shredded Muenster cheese

1. Place dried mushrooms in small bowl; cover with
   ½ cup hot water. Let stand 20 minutes or until
   softened. Drain well, reserving soaking liquid (strain
   through a fine sieve or cheesecloth if liquid is gritty.)

2. Heat oil in large skillet over medium-high heat until
   hot. Add onion; sauté 5 minutes or until lightly
   browned. Stir in tomato paste; sauté 30 seconds.
   Stir in soaked and fresh mushrooms. Sauté 6 to 8
   minutes or until mushrooms release their juices.

3. Sprinkle mushroom mixture with flour; cook
   1 minute, stirring constantly. Pour in milk and
   mushroom soaking liquid. Bring to a boil; cook
   until thickened. Season with dill, garlic salt and
   pepper. Stir in cheese until melted. Serve hot
   over pancakes.

3½ cups

SUPPER CAKE FUN FOR KIDS

For kid-friendly fun, make shapes out of the
Supper Cakes: Lay large cookie cutters (spray
inside edges with cooking spray) on the griddle
and fill with batter. Cook until set, remove cutter
and turn cakes to finish cooking.

Pizza Sauté

Pizza Sauté

½ lb. bulk Italian sausage
2 medium green or yellow bell peppers,
   cut into thin strips
1 (14½-oz.) can Italian tomato sauce
½ teaspoon fennel seeds, crushed
⅓ cup pitted kalamata olives, if desired

1. Crumble sausage into large skillet over medium-high
   heat. Sauté until sausage is no longer pink in center;
   remove from skillet, draining all but 1 tablespoon
   fat from pan. Add bell pepper strips to pan; sauté
   5 minutes or until tender.

2. Stir in tomato sauce, cooked sausage, fennel
   and olives; simmer an additional 5 minutes.
   Serve hot over pancakes.

4 cups

Family New Year's Eve

VEGETABLE SLAW WITH MINT

Seasoned rice vinegar, made with a bit of salt and sugar, makes a wonderful salad dressing. Sprinkle over sliced tomatoes or toss with baby greens. This minty slaw is fast to make and stands well.

4   cups sliced napa cabbage
1   cup shredded carrot
1   cup shredded zucchini
5   green onions, sliced
1   tablespoon chopped fresh mint
3   tablespoons seasoned rice vinegar
1   tablespoon olive oil

1. In medium bowl, combine cabbage, carrot, zucchini, green onion and mint. In small bowl, whisk vinegar and oil together. Pour over salad; toss to coat.

4 to 6 servings

Vegetable Slaw with Mint

RASPBERRY-ALMOND FUDGE PARFAITS

Big people and kids alike will love these fudgy sundaes. The chocolate sauce can be prepared ahead of time and carefully rewarmed in the microwave. Italian Amaretti cookies, or any other favorite crisp cookie, can be substituted for the biscotti.

1   cup semisweet chocolate chips
        or chocolate bar, chopped (6-oz.)
½   cup whipping cream
½   teaspoon vanilla
¼   teaspoon almond extract
8   large almond biscotti, coarsely crushed*
1   pint raspberry sorbet or sherbet
½   cup raspberry preserves, warmed

1. In small saucepan over medium-low heat, stir chocolate and cream until chocolate is melted. Remove from heat; stir until smooth. Stir in vanilla and almond extract.

2. Divide one-half of the biscotti crumbs among 4 brandy snifters or parfait glasses. Layer with sorbet, one-half of the chocolate sauce and raspberry preserves, remaining crumbs, and remaining sauce and jam. Serve immediately.

4 servings

*TIP

To crush biscotti, place in resealable plastic food storage bag; close and roll with rolling pin or pound with meat mallet until crumbled.

Raspberry-Almond Fudge Parfait

Family New Year's Eve

NEW YEAR'S DAY

Open House

by Lisa Golden Schroeder

A nice, lazy morning and all those resolutions to consider...who has time to fuss in the kitchen? New Year's Day is perfect for an easy one-dish meal, and stew fits the bill. This menu offers a nice change of scenery, shifting to the Mediterranean where the taste of warm breezes blows away the winter fog and presents a fresh new year.

Start off with a collection of easily prepared or store-bought Mediterranean "tapas"—little dishes served as appetizers—traditionally bar food in Spain, but similar to "mezes" in Greece and the Middle East. Make the Gremolata White Bean Crostini and Marinated Feta. Augment the appetizers with purchased olives, sautéed or boiled shrimp with sauces, jarred marinated

New Year's Day

Open House

Menu

Gremolata White Bean Crostini

Provencal Lamb Stew

Creamy Blue
Cheese Polenta

Marinated Feta Cheese
and Sun-Dried Tomatoes

Braised Vegetable Bouquet
with Tarragon Aioli

Cherry-Berry Clafouti

Serves 6

mushrooms or other vegetables, tapenade (olive paste), roasted garlic, or other spreads for country-style breads and toasted spiced nuts. Flavored olive oils are great for dipping crusty bread. Any of these will stand well, allowing your guests to graze throughout the day.

Make the Provencal Lamb Stew ahead of time and refrigerate or even freeze it, if you'd like. Either way, just reheat on New Year's Day and serve with the Creamy Blue Cheese Polenta. Braised winter vegetables and a baked fruit pudding finish this low-key follow-up to the previous night's celebrations.

GREMOLATA
WHITE BEAN CROSTINI

Gremolata is a fresh mixture of chopped herbs (most often parsley), lemon peel and garlic. Traditionally used to garnish stewed or roasted meats, it adds a great burst of bright flavor added to other simple foods. A gremolata can be varied by using other herbs or citrus peels (basil with orange peel, for example), but it's always distinguished by the inclusion of fresh garlic.

20 diagonally-cut slices French baguette
1 large garlic clove, halved
3 tablespoons olive oil
1 (15-oz.) can cooked white beans
     (cannellini or Great Northern)
½ to ¾ cup chicken broth
3 tablespoons finely chopped fresh Italian parsley
1 tablespoon small capers
2 teaspoons grated lemon peel
2 garlic cloves, finely chopped
½ teaspoon salt

1. Heat oven to 400°F. Rub bread slices with garlic clove halves; brush lightly using 2 tablespoon of the oil. Place on baking sheet. Toast in oven until golden brown.

2. Meanwhile, heat remaining 1 tablespoon oil in medium saucepan over medium-high heat. Add beans; sauté 4 minutes. Stir in ½ cup broth; bring to a boil. Reduce heat and simmer 2 minutes, lightly mashing beans as they cook. Remove from heat (beans should still be moist; add a bit more broth if needed).

3. Stir in parsley, capers, lemon peel and chopped garlic; season with salt to taste. Serve small spoonfuls on toasted bread.

Makes 1½ cups

PROVENCAL LAMB STEW

Herbes de Provence is a mixture of thyme, marjoram, rosemary, basil, fennel, sage and lavender—all the favorite herbs that grow in the south of France. This is a perfect dish to make ahead, freeze and rewarm on New Year's Day, saving you time to make the rest of the menu and visit with your guests.

¼ cup olive oil
3 medium onions, chopped
½ teaspoon salt
1 tablespoon red wine vinegar
2 garlic cloves, minced
1 tablespoon grated orange peel
1 teaspoon herbes de Provence or dried thyme
2 lb. lean lamb or stew beef, cut into 1-inch cubes
1½ teaspoons ground coriander
2 tablespoons all-purpose flour
3 ribs celery, cut in 1-inch pieces
1 (14½-oz.) can beef broth
¾ cup pitted prunes
½ cup ruby port wine
¾ cup pitted green olives
½ teaspoon freshly ground pepper

1. In Dutch oven, heat 2 tablespoons of the oil over medium-high heat until hot. Add onions and ¼ teaspoon of the salt. Sauté, stirring frequently, 5 minutes or until onions begin to brown. Reduce heat to low; cook and stir 6 to 8 minutes or until tender. Stir in vinegar, garlic, orange peel and herbes de Provence. Transfer to small bowl; set aside.

2. Heat oven to 350°F. Season meat with remaining ¼ teaspoon salt and coriander. Heat remaining 2 tablespoons oil in pot over medium-high heat. Add meat in batches; cook, 6 to 8 minutes per batch, turning occasionally, until meat is browned. Return meat to pan. Sprinkle meat with flour; mix well. Add celery and broth; bring to a simmer.

3. Cover pot tightly. Bake 1½ hours. Meanwhile, combine prunes and port in small bowl; set aside.

4. Add olives, onion mixture, and prunes with port to pot. Bake, covered, an additional 30 to 45 minutes or until meat is tender. Season with salt and pepper.

6 servings

A PERFECT POLENTA

Try to find the stone-ground cornmeal (available in health food stores). Regular cornmeal, which is a finer grind, will result in a softer polenta with less texture. Serve polenta freshly cooked and soft, as here, or spread it in a pan to cool. It can then be cut into squares or wedges and topped with sauces, etc.

Provencal Lamb Stew with Creamy Blue Cheese Polenta

CREAMY BLUE CHEESE POLENTA

Don't let the name polenta intimidate you—it's only cornmeal mush! It can be cut into squares or wedges and topped with sauces, etc. grated Parmesan, shredded smoked Provolone or creamy mascarpone can be substituted for the blue cheese.

4   cups water or vegetable broth
1   cup stone-ground cornmeal
½   teaspoon salt
2   tablespoons chopped fresh Italian parsley
1   tablespoon butter
½   cup crumbled blue Roquefort or Gorgonzola cheese/blue cheese

1. In large saucepan, bring water to a boil over medium-high heat. Sprinkle in cornmeal in a steady stream, stirring constantly.

2. Reduce heat to medium; cook 30 to 40 minutes, stirring frequently until polenta is thick and pulls away from side of pan. Stir in salt, parsley and butter. Serve hot, while still soft. Sprinkle each serving with cheese.

6 servings

MARINATED FETA CHEESE AND SUN-DRIED TOMATOES

Prepared ahead to allow the cheese to be flavored, the tastes of the Mediterranean shine through in this easy appetizer. If you don't have balsamic vinegar on hand, use a bit more red wine vinegar.

⅔   cup sun-dried tomatoes, cut in quarters
12 oz. feta cheese, cut into ¾-inch cubes
¼   cup thinly-sliced fresh basil leaves
3   tablespoons extra-virgin olive oil
2   tablespoons red wine vinegar
2   teaspoons balsamic vinegar
1   teaspoon freshly ground pepper
    Pita bread rounds, small focaccia bread,
      cut into wedges or crisp cracker bread

1. Place tomatoes in small bowl; add boiling water to cover. Let stand 15 minutes. Drain well.

2. Place feta and tomatoes in medium bowl. Gently stir in basil, oil, vinegars, and pepper until cheese is well coated. Cover and refrigerate at least 1 day or up to 4 days. Serve with warm pita, focaccia wedges or crisp cracker bread.

6 servings

New Year's Day Open House

BRAISED VEGETABLE BOUQUET WITH TARRAGON AIOLI

Aïóli, a mayonnaise with a lot of garlic, is a favorite condiment for vegetables in the Mediterranean. Stir in some herbs for a fun twist. If tarragon is not your favorite, try basil, chives or marjoram. Roast the garlic in the oven with the lamb stew or prepare a few days ahead and store in the refrigerator. Garnish the platter of braised vegetables with some strips of jarred roasted red pepper, if desired.

- ¾ lb. green beans
- 3 large leeks
- 3 large carrots, peeled
- 6 cups chicken broth
- ½ cup regular or light mayonnaise
- 1 tablespoon roasted garlic paste*
- 1 tablespoon finely chopped fresh tarragon leaves or 1 teaspoon dried tarragon
- 1 teaspoon grated lemon peel
- 1½ tablespoons lemon juice
- ½ teaspoon Dijon mustard
- ½ teaspoon salt

1. Trim green beans; set aside. Remove roots and outer leaves from leeks. Trim off greens to 2 inches above white part. Slice leeks in half lengthwise, not quite all the way through so that you can open leeks like a book. Wash under cold running water to remove sand and dirt; set aside. Slice carrots lengthwise into quarters, then crosswise in half.

2. Bring chicken broth to a simmer over medium heat in 12-inch-deep covered sauté pan. Lay vegetables in simmering broth. Reduce heat to medium-low; cover and cook 10 to 15 minutes or until vegetables are tender. Lift vegetables from broth with tongs; arrange attractively on serving platter. Reserve broth for another use.

3. Meanwhile, in small bowl, mix mayonnaise, garlic, tarragon, lemon peel, lemon juice and mustard. Season with salt. Serve with vegetables.

6 servings

*TIP

To roast garlic, slice top off one head of garlic, just exposing tops of cloves. Wrap head in foil; bake in 375°F oven 40 minutes or until very tender. Cool; squeeze garlic from papery skins and mash with fork. Reserve any extra garlic to serve as a spread on crusty bread with a drizzle of flavored olive oil.

CHERRY-BERRY CLAFOUTI

Clafouti, a rustic type of fruit tart, originated in France. Dark sweet cherries are traditional, topped with a pancake-like custard batter that puffs when it's baked. Clafouti is best served warm, dusted with powdered sugar, complemented by ice cream or whipped cream. Here, a refreshing lemon sorbet complements the vanilla-scented fruit. Kirsch, a cherry-flavored brandy from France, or another favorite fruit liqueur (blackberry brandy, Grand Marnier or Courvoisier) would be a delicious addition to this simple dessert: add a tablespoon or two to the batter poured over the fruit.

- 2 cups frozen dark sweet pitted cherries, thawed
- 1 cup mixed frozen berries (raspberries, blackberries, blueberries), thawed
- ¾ cup sugar
- 2 teaspoons cornstarch
- ½ cup all-purpose flour
- ⅛ teaspoon salt
- 3 eggs
- 1 cup milk
- 2 teaspoons vanilla
  Powdered sugar
- 2 pints lemon sorbet

1. Heat oven to 400°F. Generously butter 10-inch pie plate. In medium bowl, combine cherries and berries. Stir ¼ cup of the sugar and cornstarch into fruits and juices. Transfer mixture to pie plate.

2. In medium bowl, stir together remaining ½ cup sugar, flour and salt. Whisk in eggs, milk and vanilla until batter is smooth. Pour batter over fruit. Bake 30 to 35 minutes or until edges are well-puffed and golden brown. Sprinkle with powdered sugar. Serve warm with scoops of sorbet.

8 servings

Braised Vegetable Bouquet with Tarragon Aiôli

Cherry-Berry Clafouti

178

NEW YEAR'S DAY

Bowl Party

by John Schumacher

It's sort of a shame all the New Year's attention gets focused on the evening before the actual day. Why not make something grand and wonderful for New Year's Day festivities, such as watching football games or just an old-fashioned get-together?

This menu offers a host of flavors which bring anticipation for New Year's Day. Kabobs are easy to prepare ahead, then broil to order. The seafood and mushrooms in the pizza, and the roasted vegetables, are a sound base to build on for the start of the New Year. The Champagne Slush is light and exciting, and imparts a true sense of adventure.

NEW YEAR'S DAY

Bowl Party

MENU

YEAR LONG KABOBS

BURGUNDY BARBECUE DEMI-GLACE

CRAB AND SHRIMP PORTOBELLO
MUSHROOM PIZZA WITH ROASTED
GARLIC MASHED POTATOES

BUFFALO SWEET AND SAUERBRATEN

OVEN-ROASTED VEGETABLES

CHAMPAGNE SLUSH WITH ORANGE
LIQUEUR DIPPING SAUCE

Serves 8

These dishes can be served in any space—such as a dining room table, kitchen counter, television trays or a rolling cart. Use as many brightly-colored serving dishes as you can muster.

All these recipes can be prepared one to two days in advance, leaving time for good cheer on New Year's Eve, and sleep on New Year's Day before the festivities begin again.

Year Long Kabobs and Burgandy Barbeque Demi-Glace

YEAR LONG KABOBS

The 13 ingredients represent each month of the year, plus one extra to begin the new year. The flavor takes you through all four seasons and with each morsel removed, you need to reflect on a special event of the year. The last hot pepper will give you a flaming start on the new year.

2 cups barbecue sauce
1 quart chicken stock
2 bay leaves
1 teaspoon freshly ground pepper
1 teaspoon fennel seeds
1 teaspoon minced garlic
4 smoked Polish sausages, whole
4 sweet Italian sausages, whole
4 zucchini squash
4 carrots
2 large red bell peppers, seeded, cut in quarters
2 large yellow bell peppers, seeded, cut in quarters
8 (6-inch) ribs celery, peeled
4 leeks
4 large mushroom caps

4 boneless skinless chicken breast halves
1 large honeydew melon
4 jumbo dill pickles
8 long bamboo skewers
4 jalapeño peppers
4 sweet baby gherkins
   Burgundy-Barbecue Demi-Glace

1. In large heavy pot, combine barbecue sauce, chicken stock, bay leaves, pepper, fennel seeds and garlic; bring to a slow rolling boil. Add whole sausages, squash, carrots, peppers, celery, leeks, mushroom caps and chicken breasts. Simmer on low heat 5 minutes. Remove pot from heat; set on rack. Let stock and kabob ingredients cool to room temperature in pot.

2. With tongs, remove all kabob ingredients to baking sheet. Keep all like ingredients together for assembly. Remove stem and seeds from jalapeño peppers. Stuff each jalapeño pepper with sweet baby gherkin.

3. Cut sausages, squash, carrots, celery, and dill pickles lengthwise. Cut honeydew melon in half. Remove seeds and rind. Slice into 1-inch wide slices. Skewer items in the following order with one skewer: mushroom cap, carrot, celery, red bell pepper, polish sausage, leek, chicken breast, melon, zucchini squash, dill pickle, Italian sausage, yellow bell pepper, jalapeño pepper. Lay skewer flat on table and gently run second bamboo skewer through other side. Remember not all items are the same length, so make sure to leave at least one inch at the end. Add stuffed jalapeño pepper and mushroom cap to remaining skewer tip.

4. Heat grill. Spray or brush kabobs lightly with olive oil. Cook on gas grill over medium heat or on charcoal grill 4 to 6 inches from medium coals until sausage and chicken are no longer pink in center.

5. With very sharp, thin knife, cut between two skewers to make 8 individual kabobs. Stack in warm chafing dish. Serve with hot Burgundy-Barbecue Demi-Glace (recipe below).

8 kabobs

BURGUNDY BARBEQUE DEMI-GLACE

Reducing one-quart of red wine to one cup intensifies the flavor 12 times. Covered with barbecue sauce it heightens your senses. It is bold enough to access each of the 13 ingredients in Year Long Kabobs and still not lose its identity.

4   cups Burgundy wine
2   cups barbecue sauce
½   teaspoon white pepper

1. In heavy saucepan, over medium-high heat, reduce wine to 1 cup. Add barbecue sauce and white pepper; reduce heat. Simmer wine, sauce and pepper over low heat 5 minutes. Serve with Year Long Kabobs.

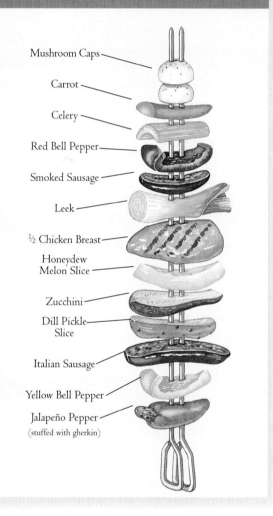

MAKING THE KABOBS

Twelve ingredients represent each month of the past year, and one extra hot pepper starts the new year with a BANG! Here's how to organize your kabobs:

Mushroom Caps

Carrot

Celery

Red Bell Pepper

Smoked Sausage

Leek

½ Chicken Breast

Honeydew Melon Slice

Zucchini

Dill Pickle Slice

Italian Sausage

Yellow Bell Pepper

Jalapeño Pepper
(stuffed with gherkin)

ROASTED GARLIC MASHED POTATOES

Create these potatoes to use on Crab and Shrimp Portobello Mushroom Pizza.

⅓ cup whole garlic cloves, peeled
½ cup butter
I to 2 teaspoons whipping cream
4 to 6 russet potatoes, washed thoroughly, peeled or unpeeled, cut into quarters
I tablespoon salt
½ cup butter
¼ cup whipping cream
I teaspoon salt
¼ teaspoon freshly ground white pepper

1. Heat oven to 325°F. Place garlic cloves and ½ cup butter in small pan. Cover and bake I hour or until garlic is soft. In blender, combine garlic and liquid; puree, adding cream if needed to make smooth consistency. Garlic puree can be prepared days in advance. Store covered in glass jar in refrigerator.

2. In large pot, cover potatoes with cold water; add salt. Boil slowly until potatoes are tender when pierced with thin paring knife. Drain off water. Let potatoes stand, covered, 5 minutes. Add butter, cream, salt, pepper and roasted garlic puree. Mash until creamy.

8 servings

CRAB AND SHRIMP PORTOBELLO MUSHROOM PIZZA

There is always a sense of anticipation when one thinks of crab, shrimp and mushrooms. Serving it on a pizza crust keeps the light, playful spirit of the New Year's Day football games. This recipe could be a meal in itself.

4 cups Roasted Garlic Mashed Potatoes (recipe at left)

Sauce
4 tablespoons butter
I cup shallots, cut into ¼-inch-thick pieces
2 garlic cloves, minced
2 cups fresh crimini mushrooms, sliced ¼-inch-thick
4 tablespoons flour
I teaspoon salt
¼ teaspoon freshly ground white pepper
½ teaspoon dry mustard
I teaspoon fresh lemon juice
2 cups dry white wine
I teaspoon Worcestershire sauce
8 egg yolks
2 cups whipping cream
½ cup tomato puree

Crust
4 cups warm water (I05-II5°F)
4 tablespoons active dry yeast or 4 (¼-oz.) pkg. active dry yeast
2 teaspoons sugar
4 teaspoons salt
4 tablespoons vegetable oil
I0 to I2 cups all-purpose flour
I teaspoon freshly ground pepper
2 teaspoons dried basil

Mushrooms
8 portobello mushrooms
¼ cup olive oil
I cup Marsala wine
24 cooked large green shrimp, peeled, tails on
I½ lb. cooked whole crab legs, cut into 2-inch pieces
½ cup freshly grated Parmesan cheese (2-oz.)

Crab and Shrimp Portobello Mushroom Pizza (with Roasted Garlic Mashed Potatoes)

1. Prepare Roasted Garlic Mashed Potatoes. Set aside.

2. To prepare sauce, in large skillet, heat butter over medium-high heat until melted; add shallots. Cook until clear and tender (do not brown). Add garlic and mushrooms; simmer 2 minutes, stirring gently. Combine flour, salt, pepper and dry mustard. Sprinkle evenly over sauce; very gently stir into butter mixture. When lumps are gone, add lemon juice, white wine and Worcestershire sauce. Simmer 3 minutes. In small bowl, combine egg yolks, cream and tomato puree. Slowly add ½ cup hot wine mixture to cream mixture. Stir together; slowly pour back into wine mixture. Stir with wooden spoon to make smooth, rich sauce. Remove from heat and cover.

3. To prepare pizza crust, in large bowl, combine warm water, yeast and sugar; let stand 2 minutes. Add salt and oil. In another large bowl, combine 9¾ cups flour, pepper and basil. Add one-half of flour mixture to yeast mixture. With large wooden spoon, mix 20 times. Gradually add remaining flour mixture, ½ cup at a time, until dough forms mass and pulls away from sides of bowl. Remove dough to floured baking cloth. Add remaining ¼ cup flour. Knead dough 50 times, adding more flour a little at a time. Place in greased bowl; cover with clean cloth. Set in a warm (not hot) place for one hour.

4. Meanwhile, prepare portobello mushrooms. Remove stems and wash mushrooms. In large skillet, heat olive oil over medium-high heat until hot. Add mushrooms top side down; sauté 1 minute. Turn caps. Add Marsala wine and simmer 3 minutes. Lay mushrooms open side up on aluminum foil-lined baking sheet. Using pastry bag with star tip, pipe garlic mashed potatoes around edge of each mushroom to make decorative border. Place 3 cooked shrimp head-to-tail around inside edge of mashed potatoes. Equally divide cooked crab pieces and place in center of each mushroom. Top each mushroom with ¾ cup sauce. Sprinkle Parmesan cheese over top of each mushroom. Cover and refrigerate.

5. When pizza dough has risen, punch down; knead 5 times. Heat oven to 400°F. Divide dough into 8 equal portions. Press each piece into small round crust on baking sheet. Bake 15 minutes or until crusts are golden brown and crisp. Do not overbake crusts or they will become bitter.

6. To assemble pizzas, remove prepared mushrooms from refrigerator. Reduce oven temperature to 375°F. Bake mushrooms 10 minutes. Place stuffed mushrooms on precooked pizza crust; bake 15 minutes.

8 individual pizzas

BUFFALO SWEET
AND SAUERBRATEN

Buffalo has a sense of strength. Sweet and sour is how most years unfold for us. Together this marriage of flavors keys into all your senses. It gives a feeling of pending adventure.

Marinade

2 cups cold beef stock
1 tablespoon beef base
1½ cups red wine vinegar
1½ cups Burgundy wine
1 cup thinly sliced onions
½ cup thinly sliced carrots
½ cup thinly sliced celery
2 tablespoons packed brown sugar
2 garlic cloves, chopped
1 teaspoon salt
2 bay leaves
6 crushed black peppercorns
4 whole cloves
1 tablespoon juniper berries
1½ cups diced tomatoes with juice

Meat

1 (4-lb.) boneless buffalo roast or boneless beef roast
⅓ cup vegetable oil
1 cup crushed gingersnap cookies
⅔ cup raisins
2 cups fresh pineapple, cut in ½-inch cubes

1. In large bowl, combine beef stock and base, vinegar, wine, onions, carrots, celery, brown sugar, garlic, slat, bay leaves, peppercorns, cloves, berries, and tomatoes with juice; mix until well blended.

2. Remove all fat and silver skin from buffalo meat. Pierce meat at random with boning knife. Place meat in glass or stainless steel bowl; cover with marinade. Cover bowl. Refrigerate 72 hours. If you marinate for less than 72 hours, buffalo will be tough. If you marinate more than 72 hours, meat will become dry and flavorless.

3. Heat oven to 375°F. Remove meat from marinade; pat dry. In large skillet, heat oil over medium-high heat until hot. Cook meat until brown on all sides. Transfer meat to large ovenproof pot; add

marinade. Bake, covered, 2½ hours or until meat thermometer reaches 180°F. When meat is done, transfer to dry pan. Cover with damp cloth to keep warm.

4. Remove bay leaves from liquid. In blender, combine marinade and vegetables; puree. Pour puree into heavy pot; whisk cookies into liquid, stirring until smooth. Add raisins and pineapple; simmer 5 minutes. Slice meat across grain into 1-inch-thick pieces; cover with hot marinade.

About 8 servings

OVEN-ROASTED VEGETABLES

These vegetables are easy to prepare, easy to eat and easy to like! It gives a sense of stability.

8 carrots
8 parsnips
8 red potatoes
8 turnips
8 plum tomatoes
¼ cup olive oil
1 cup seasoned flour*

1. Heat oven to 375°F. Peel carrots, parsnips, potatoes and turnips with potato peeler. Remove stem ends from tomatoes.

2. Line baking pan with aluminum foil; lightly brush bottom with olive oil. Lightly brush vegetables except tomatoes with olive oil. Roll in seasoned flour; arrange on pan about 1 inch apart; bake 30 minutes. Gently turn vegetables; add tomatoes and bake an additional 20 minutes.

8 servings

* TIP

Seasoned flour is a combination of 1 cup all-purpose flour, 2 teaspoons salt and ⅛ teaspoon white pepper.

CHAMPAGNE SLUSH WITH ORANGE LIQUEUR DIPPING SAUCE

The title says it all: celebration, youth and easy living. This recipe is a fun way to end the day.

Slush

¾ cup freshly-squeezed lemon juice
½ cup cold water
2 cups sugar
2 cups club soda, chilled
1 bottle sparkling wine, chilled

Sugared Fruit

Jumbo strawberries (stems on)
Fresh pineapple slices
Melon slices (skins removed)
Kiwi slices
Apple slices
Pear slices
Banana slices
Orange medallions
½ cup packed brown sugar

Orange Liqueur Dipping Sauce

1 cup sour cream
1 cup lemon yogurt
⅔ cup currant jelly
¼ cup Grand Marnier
1 tablespoon arrowroot

Champagne Slush

1. Squeeze lemons; strain through coffee strainer, then through coffee filter. Squeeze 1¼ cups lemon juice to end up with ¾ cup double-strained juice.

2. In small heavy saucepan, heat lemon juice, water and sugar over high heat; boil 1 minute. Remove from heat; let cool and refrigerate until chilled.

3. Freeze 2 baking sheets. In large chilled bowl, combine chilled wine, lemon-sugar mixture and club soda. Pour onto frozen baking sheets.

4. Place pans on flat shelf in freezer; freeze 30 minutes. Pull fork through the frozen liquid to make slush. Repeat every 30 minutes until slush is firm. Remove from baking sheet; store frozen in tightly covered container. To serve, freeze stemmed glassed. Divide slush evenly among glasses. Serve with Sugared Fruit and Orange Liqueur Dipping Sauce.

5. To prepare Sugared Fruit, wash fruit and remove stems or peels. Remove all white membranes from peeled fruit. Combine fruit; top with brown sugar. Cover with plastic wrap; refrigerate.

6. To prepare Orange Liqueur Dipping Sauce, in blender, combine sour cream, yogurt, jelly, orange liqueur and cornstarch; puree at medium speed 1 minute. Pour mixture into large saucepan; heat to boiling over medium heat. Reduce heat to low; simmer 2 minutes, stirring constantly. Pour into bowl; cover with plastic wrap. Poke holes in film with toothpick to let out steam and heat.

7. Place sugared fruit in a chilled serving dish and dipping sauce in a shallow serving bowl. On a serving tray place frozen slush-filled glasses accompanied with ice teaspoons, fruit and dipping sauce.

CHEF JOHN'S NOTES ON SLUSH

Any sparkling wine works well.

If you wish the tart flavor of Champagne, use an extra dry Champagne.

To use expensive Champagne is counter-productive, as the lemon syrup overwhelms the delicate flavor.

You may freeze the lemon mixture in ice cube trays and add to tall drinks.

My favorite way to prepare this recipe is with Asti Spumanti.

For children, prepare with sparkling grape juice.

New Year's Day Bowl Party

INDEX